THE WEALTH MANAGEMENT INDEX™

The Financial Advisor's System for Assessing & Managing Your Client's Plans & Goals

ROSS LEVIN, CFP

Irwin/IAFP Series in Financial Planning

INTERNATIONAL ASSOCIATION
FOR FINANCIAL PLANNING

Chicago • London • Singapore

To my daughters Vera and Mimi,
I love you forever and like you always

Irwin/McGraw-Hill

A Division of The McGraw·Hill Companies

Wealth Management Index™ is a trademark of R. Levin/Accredited Investors Inc.

This publication is designed to provide accurate and authoritative information in regard to the subject matter covered. It is sold with the understanding that neither the author nor the publisher is engaged in rendering legal, accounting, or other professional service. If legal advice or other expert assistance is required, the services of a competent professional person should be sought.

From a Declaration of Principles jointly adopted by a Committee of the American Bar Association and a Committee of Publishers.

Library of Congress Cataloging-in-Publication Data
Levin, Ross.
    The wealth management index : the financial advisor's system for assessing & managing your client's plans & goals / Ross Levin.
      p. cm.
    Includes index.
    ISBN 0-7863-1020-0
    1. Financial planners– –United States. 2. Financial services industry– –United States. I. Title.
HG179.5.L48   1997
332.6—dc20   96–34668

Printed in the United States of America

   5 6 7 8 9   BKM BKM   0 9 8 7 6 5 4 3

INTRODUCTION

As an active advocate of the financial planning industry since I started in the field in 1982, I see us at a crossroads. The direction we take will determine whether we become a profession. I frankly am concerned with what I see and hope to be able to redirect us back onto the path that was illuminated so brightly in the mid-1980s.

This book is for financial planners. This is a book for those people who talk to their clients daily about how they can reach their financial dreams while averting financial disappointment. This book is to help all of us to *remember* who we are rather than to *redefine* who we are.

Who we are is immutable. How our clients define what they want may be transitional. We want to help our clients understand and, more important, make a commitment to what they want. This commitment will be made with us and will be guided by us, but it is not a task that may be delegated. We need to bring our reality into our clients' commitment through a holistic approach.

To illustrate the danger of compartmentalization, I offer the following scenario. Two moose hunters were dropped off via float plane by their outfitter. When the outfitter returned in 3 days, he helped them pack up all their gear for their return flight over the densely tree-covered, sparsely populated land.

Hunter 1 asked, "Aren't you going to strap the two moose we shot on the plane?"

The guide said, "We would never be able to get the plane off the water."

Hunter 2 said, "But we did it last year."

The guide reluctantly tied a moose onto each of the plane's pontoons. He started at the far end of the lake and gunned the plane. After almost a mile of taxiing, the plane barely got out of the water, narrowly missed the first set of trees and went crashing into a large tree only 100 yards off the lake.

Hunter 1 was laying in a clump 30 feet from the plane, while hunter 2 found himself lodged in a tree.

Hunter 1 called, "Where are we?"

Hunter 2 looked around and yelled back, "Fifty feet further than last year."

Too often, we focus our clients on those last 50 feet. We direct our clients' attention to some of the least significant benefits that we offer and divert their attention from reaching their long-term goals. This is a book about a recommitment to what we do better than any other professionals in the world—help people evaluate their current situation, establish appropriate objectives, set up a plan, implement that plan, and monitor the results. If we are not doing this for our clients, we are not doing a good job for ourselves or our profession.

The difficulty lies in creating a method for developing with our clients a system of monitoring that is tangible; that is, a system that can be scored annually and where progress is noted. Most important, the system must address the critical areas of financial planning in a manner such that the less exotic planning concepts do not get ignored.

The Wealth Management Index™ is a tool that my business partner and I developed for our firm, Accredited Investors, Inc., in Minneapolis. It has been refined by my friends in the Alpha Group, a consortium of 15 planners from around the country who are dedicated to wealth management for their clients and committed to building the financial planning profession. This index will be instrumental in helping you gauge your performance as a financial planner against the only relevant benchmark there is—your clients' unique needs.

Wealth Management Index™ is a trademark of R. Levin/Accredited Investors Inc.

After reading this, you will not only have a formula to measure your clients' successes, but you will also have a formula to retain satisfied clients. The Wealth Management Index manages client expectations. In a rapidly changing, information-filled world, expectation management is critical in helping clients meet their objectives because it keeps them focused on those objectives.

Ross Levin

ACKNOWLEDGMENTS

My wife Bridget gave me a Ziggy cartoon several months ago that I have prominently displayed on my desk. Ziggy is being x-rayed at the doctor's office and the results show a novel wedged deep inside his belly. The doctor says, "You have a book inside of you." Writing this book has, at times, probably felt like what Ziggy must go through to purge his system of his writings. But it sure feels good when it's done.

I could not have begun to do this without the support of several people, none being more instrumental than Bridget. Not only did she help plant the seed for the Wealth Management Index by telling my partner and I that we need some tangible way to show clients their broad success in financial planning, but she served as my inspiration when I was too tired to write, my confidante when I expressed my fears around being published, my editor who was unashamed to set me straight, and my beacon when I found myself buried in the forest of this project. I am eternally grateful and express my devotion to her publicly.

My business partner, Wil Heupel, has also helped bring the Wealth Management Index to life in our practice. His workplan concept described in the book has helped us to focus on our client needs in a way that is easy to track. He has been a friend and a pillar of strength throughout our eight-year partnership.

Amy Ost, my editor at Irwin, took all my phone calls—even when she knew it was me. She put up with my idiosyncrasies, bolstered my confidence, and even understood what I was writing. Any usefulness from this project is a tribute to her.

Other people and institutions were critical to this book. The International Association for Financial Planning's (as well as

NAPFA's and the ICFP's) conferences and meetings gave me tremendous contacts from whom I could glean information. Eleanor Blayney, Harold Evensky, Mark Balasa, and the whole Alpha Group helped me with many of the concepts used here. Many of the professionals that we use in our practice—the attorneys, accountants, business managers, and bankers—were constant sources for technical answers. Tracy Hunt provided much needed sourcing.

Writing a book is a humbling experience. I cast my ideas out to you, hoping you will take what applies and find them useful, recognizing that you can inevitably improve upon them, and thanking you for granting me your time to read my words.

R. L.

CONTENTS

1

THE WEALTH MANAGEMENT INDEX™

The concept of wealth management is rooted in the belief that financial planning is a process. This process begins when the client first comes into your office with his or her completed information-gathering form and theoretically ends only when the client passes away. Throughout this lifetime client relationship, we try to make sure that everything that we do is congruent with a planner's only reason for being—to help that client reach his or her personal financial objectives.

Practically, though, those objectives are always changing. While our clients' core beliefs often hold firm, the diverse goals expressed to us change frequently. Planning involves helping our clients to continually assess those goals, to set new priorities with them if they are divergent, and to execute strategies to help attain them.

Many of us treat financial planning for our clients as though we are training for a marathon. The information-gathering and

---

Wealth Management Index™ is a trademark of R. Levin/Accredited Investors Inc.

goal-setting meeting is like buying new running shoes and clothing. The actual plan compares with our training log. The actual race is our implementation. And like running a marathon, if we do nothing else after the race is over, our financial stomachs begin to protrude over our belt and in only a few months we must pause as we climb our personal financial steps. Financial planning without ongoing monitoring and adjusting is like running a marathon once and believing that you are going to be in great shape for the rest of your life.

This problem often arises because of the nature of the planning relationship. Clients often come to us because they feel as if some aspect of their financial life is out of control. This discomfort makes them willing to accept the sometimes painful process of looking at their entire situation on paper. This discomfort is the catalyst for engaging us.

As planners, we do everything in our power to recognize this discomfort and treat it. If we do a good job, our clients begin to feel better about their circumstances and the unease disappears. Eventually, the clients forget what made them uncomfortable in the first place. At this point, clients continue to work with us only because they like us or because we are performing some functional task. Both of these reasons mask our true value.

We often tell clients that the bulk of our planning work was handled in year 1. We offer incidental financial planning advice as we begin to perform other ongoing tasks for our clients, like asset management. Ironically, the ongoing tasks may actually be the *cause* of new discomfort.

We begin to focus our clients on those functions that are most visible and seemingly most dynamic. Rather than continuing to have the clients grasp the total wealth management ring, we may have them focus solely on the asset management pony as their financial objective carousel spins round and round until the music (maybe it's mediocre short-term performance) stops. The "results" of individual components of the financial plan, when viewed out of context, are at best deceiving and at worst, meaningless.

While our clients initially focused on the total plan, we inadvertently shifted them to important, but not nearly complete, components of the plan. We all know, for example, that in a roaring US bull market, a properly allocated portfolio is destined to trail most of the US indices. We have chosen to accept this because in the context of the financial plan, an appropriate risk-adjusted portfolio tied into the client's objectives is more meaningful than absolute total return. Yet we often confuse asset allocation with money management. We don't try to maximize total returns but only risk-adjusted returns.

In a world dominated by short-term performance numbers, if we bill ourselves as money managers, then this is clearly a precursor to failure. Of course our clients would become confused or disenchanted by this. Not only are we no longer (through the client's eyes) providing the broad range of service for which we were originally hired, but we are also focusing all the client's attention on something whose importance is directly tied to the successful completion of the other areas.

Financial planning is not an event. It is a never-ending process of adjustments and re-evaluations. Unfortunately, both we and our clients can lose sight of this as we begin to focus on individual components of our strategy, like investment performance, rather than on our comprehensive goal of tying total wealth management into stated client objectives.

The Wealth Management Index was created so that we can regularly measure our clients' progress through the myriad of financial goals and decisions they make and *do not make*. The index supports flexibility and change. It evolves every year and is communicated to the client. The index helps us to *manage expectations* by continuing to focus the relationship on all of the client's stated goals and objectives.

The index should not be used in isolation. It must be integrated with a client workplan to encourage the maximum opportunity for success. A workplan is essentially an outline you prepare with the client that details how you are going to work together and how success will be measured. It will include an expectation around client service as well as a summary of the key areas that need to be concentrated on within the Wealth Management Index. Through agreement on the workplan, you can ensure that you will validate the subsequent results of the index.

ACCREDITED INVESTORS' WEALTH MANAGEMENT INDEX

The Wealth Management Index is a tool to quantify a client's annual success toward reaching his or her stated ends. Since we are concerned about total wealth accumulation, preservation, and distribution, many important areas are included.

The index has five major categories and several subcategories within each major category.

Index Percentage for Each Category

The percentage of the Wealth Management Index assigned to each of the five categories follows:

25%	Asset protection (preservation).
20%	Disability and income protection (protection).
10%	Debt management (leverage).
25%	Investment and cash flow planning (accumulation).
20%	Estate planning (distribution).

Measurement is against targets developed jointly with the client and outlined within a workplan. One does not measure against indexes. Each year, measurement is against the overall success of the weighted objectives in the Wealth Management Index which is laid out at the annual review. These mutually developed and agreed-upon objectives then form the only relevant basis for judging success. Focus must logically move to the comprehensive index.

The individual parts of the index are integrated within categories and among categories. Obviously cash flow analysis for the retiree is somewhat dependent upon investment planning and asset protection must be entwined with estate planning. Since we measure success within categories, each area is judged against the developed benchmarks. These areas scored independently create the success in the integrated and interdependent financial plan.

Undoubtedly certain areas will be seemingly more important to different clients, but that does not minimize the significance of the other areas. Most of your work with the client will be on the components in which he or she feels a deficiency. That does not mean that the other components should be ignored. In fact, it is the affirmation of success in these other areas that will allow you to focus on the other concerns you have exposed.

There are a tremendous number of issues related to financial planning. These issues are often very difficult to keep track of. As you use the Wealth Management Index, you may wish to incorporate a checklist system to ensure that you are covering all relevant topics. Ed Morrow, a financial planner in Youngstown, Ohio, has developed a checklist program within his comprehensive Text Library System (offered through both the International Association for Financial Planning and the Institute of Certified Financial Planners) that you may find quite useful.

As you go through the components of the Wealth Management Index, it will be obvious that all aspects of financial planning fall under at least one of the following five major categories. The subcategories and their respective percentages of the Wealth Management Index are also given in further detail.

Subcategories and Percentage Allocations

1. Asset Protection (Preservation)

Percentage allocation within category

34%	Are your business interests adequately covered?
33%	Do you have an appropriate amount of life insurance consistent with an articulated philosophy around this insurance?
33%	Have you protected yourself against catastrophic loss due to long-term care, property losses, or liability issues?

2. Disability and Income Protection (Protection)

Percentage allocation within category

40%	Do you have too much or too little disability protection given your assets and income, and will it pay you should you be unable to work?
20%	Did you receive in income from all sources (earnings, gifts, social security, pensions) what you expected to this year?
20%	Did you spend according to plan?
20%	Did you use all reasonable means to reduce your taxes?

3. Debt Management (Leverage)

Percentage allocation within category

40%	Is your current ratio stronger than 2:1 and is your total debt reasonable as a percentage of your total assets?
10%	Is your debt tax-efficient?
30%	Have you access to as much debt as reasonably possible and at the best available rates?
20%	Have you managed your debt as expected?

4. Investment Planning (Accumulation)

Percentage allocation within category

10%	How did you do against your established rate-of-return target (CPI plus stated percentage)?
40%	Were your annual contributions or withdrawals at target?
40%	Is your asset allocation appropriate?
5%	Was the portfolio income tax-efficient?
5%	Have you set aside enough cash for anticipated purchases in the next 3 years?

5. Estate Planning (Distribution)

Percentage allocation within category

40%	Does your will match your wealth transfer wishes?

15%	Do you need and have
	◆ A power of attorney?
	◆ A health care declaration?
	◆ A living will?
25%	Are your assets titled correctly and are all beneficiary designations appropriate?
15%	Have you established and funded all necessary trusts?
5%	Have you made your desired gifts for this year?

Individual Components and Percentage Allocations

The 21 individual components of the Wealth Management Index represent the following percentage of the total scale:

1.	Is your asset allocation appropriate?	10%
2.	Were your annual contributions or withdrawals at target?	10%
3.	Are your business interests adequately covered?	8.5%
4.	Do you have an appropriate amount of life insurance, consistent with an articulated philosophy around this insurance?	8.25%
5.	Have you protected yourself against catastrophic loss due to long-term care, property losses, or liability issues?	8.25%
6.	Does your will match your wealth transfer wishes?	8%
7.	Do you have too much or too little disability protection given your assets and income and will it pay you should you be unable to work?	8%

8. Are your assets titled correctly and are all beneficiary designations appropriate?   5%

9. Did you receive in income from all sources (earnings, gifts, social security, pension) what you expected to this year?   4%

10. Did you use all reasonable means to reduce your taxes?   4%

11. Did you spend according to plan?   4%

12. Is your current ratio better than 2:1 and is your total debt reasonable as a percentage of your assets?   4%

13. Have you established and funded all necessary trusts?   3%

14. Do you need and have a power of attorney, a health care declaration, or a living will?   3%

15. Have you access to as much debt as reasonably possible and at the best available rates?   3%

16. How did your rate of return compare with the CPI?   2.5%

17. Have you managed your debt as expected?   2%

18. Have you set aside enough cash for purchases to be made in the next 3 years?   1.25%

19. Was the portfolio income tax-efficient?   1.25%

20. Is your debt tax-efficient?   1%

21. Have you made your desired gifts for this year?   1%

It is important to note that no single item has a weighted value greater than 10 percent. This clearly reinforces the many facets of financial planning that come into play in developing an effective strategy. I would also suggest that planners tend to spend a disproportionate amount of meeting and service time in areas with relatively low overall weightings but high visibility, thereby ignoring some of the other key areas in a plan. This would be akin to a business lawyer focusing every meeting back to the company's articles of incorporation rather than to the constantly evolving legal needs of the business in the context of an overall plan.

Scoring

Each year, you would score your client on a 10-point scale within each category. The point total is then multiplied by the percent within category to give you points toward the index. All of these points are then added up to give your client his or her total Wealth Management Index score.

Total points scored and their significance

85–100	Financial plan should meet your objectives.
65–84	Financial plan needs to be more focused on your needs.
Under 65	Planning overhaul is necessary.

At every annual review, you will score with the client the components of the Wealth Management Index. The successes should be noted; the areas in which the client did not score high need to be a focus the following year.

The scoring may seem relatively narrow. *The Wealth Management Index cannot be scored on a curve. It is not a relative scale to be compared among clients. The objective is for each client to be successful in reaching his or her objectives.*

As you score the Wealth Management Index with the client, you will create a whole new set of talking points. Values may be redefined. The reason the client needs to be part of the scoring process is because it brings the index down to an emotional level—a level that will help the client to see how he or she is vulnerable.

There are more subtle, but extremely important , benefits that are experienced as you work with the client on the Wealth Management Index. You will have clearly aligned yourself as the client's advocate. You will have assessed honestly with the client his or her situation, and you will have taken joint responsibility for the financial plan's effectiveness. The client will then be engaged in the plan with you. This interdependence will help to cultivate the long-term relationship we all seek to have with our clients.

The rest of the book is set up to help guide you through the workplan and each component of the Wealth Management Index and to provide strategic decisions around each element. It will serve as a critical guide and checklist for comprehensively servicing your clients' needs.

2

ESTABLISHING THE RELATIONSHIP

The Wealth Management Index exists only as a tool to measure the progress that our clients are making toward their dreams. Our job is not only to help people realize their dreams, but it is also to fundamentally help them begin to dream in the first place.

We serve a tremendously useful purpose by helping people create and realize their visions for themselves. Concomitantly, we have to help modulate those lofty visions to provide a solid grounding. But dreams help people live rather than merely exist. We are life enhancers because we are dream realizers.

GETTING TO KNOW YOUR CLIENT

How do we find out what is most important to our clients? We have to begin by listening without asking. Our job is to go beyond what the clients tell us to try to develop an even deeper level of understanding. A fact-finding, information-gathering, write-down-your-dreams form is as limiting as it is overwhelming. The initial interview is a minuet. The relationship develops almost rhythmically; two (or three) people carefully try to gain confidence in each other. A somewhat uncomfortable prospect must be made to feel at ease by your ability to *hear what he or she isn't saying.*

An initial meeting must be first a dialogue, not a monologue. It is not the time to throw down the Ibbotson charts and spew modern portfolio theory; it is a meeting of intense listening and replaying to the client exactly what you heard. The relationship begins not when you show the client everything that you know, but rather when you show the client you want to get to know *them.* Steven Covey in his *Seven Habits of Highly Effective People* says you should "first seek to understand, then to be understood."[1]

As you encourage the client to talk and to share, you begin to get a feeling about what expectations are, what the client is most afraid of, and what success will look like. Some useful questions that we incorporate into our initial meetings are given and explained below.

What Money Messages Did You Get Growing Up? We are all creatures of our past so this simple question allows people to discuss how their family background shaped their money profile. It's amazing how frequently people will recognize that many of their feelings surrounding money evolved around the dinner table. This question also invites additional questions regarding perceived obligations to parents as they age. Watch closely as you ask this question to discover the depth and type of feelings around money.

---

[1] Steven R. Covey, *Seven Habits of Highly Effective People* (New York: Simon and Schuster, 1989).

If I Were to Do a Great Job for You, What Would That Look Like? How Would You Feel About Your Situation? This expectation question is central to developing a wealth management program and workplan revolving around the client's perceived needs. As you delve into other areas, remember that this original answer depicts the things which the client has expressed in his or her stated objectives. While we will most likely discover and plan around other important areas, we cannot choose to minimize the original expectations laid out for us. As we work on the things that we have uncovered, we need to get client consensus on the importance of these items.

What Do You See as Your Level of Involvement in This Process? This will help you identify the client's profile and understand how he or she learns. A follow-up question can be *"How do you like information presented to you?"* Some clients are extremely visual and can learn more from charts and graphs than from pure text. Some clients want significant supporting information. Some clients don't look at the printed word or pictures at all and simply choose to listen to what you are saying.

What Is Important About Money (or Success) to You? This came directly from Bill Bachrach who runs a sales consulting practice in San Diego and is a popular national speaker. This question needs to be asked over again based on the response you get. For example, if the response is "it gives me options," then ask, "What is important about options to you?" Most clients have not really thought that deeply about what money means to them. This line of questioning gets you amazingly close to your clients because it is engaging and nonjudgmental. It also helps you sift through a lot of data to get down to the issue of fundamental needs or values.

Determining Client Profiles

Surprisingly, we need to overlay the identity of the individual client into a framework of client phenotypes to help us better understand how to communicate and craft suitable plans. While planning is individual, it is inconceivable that one can build a successful practice without some amount of standard operating procedures.

My firm works with high-income, high-net-worth clients. They derive their wealth from a number of different occupations. They have a broad range of feelings about money and, irrespective of their age, their goals and objectives are unique and personal. Our clients are unique—just like everyone else! In spite of their individuality, they also have some core similarities. To build a robust practice, you need to standardize around those similarities yet be flexible enough to recognize and deliver to the uniquenesses.

One useful concept that I have found is understanding client profiles. While clients within each profile may be dissimilar, their interaction with me or my partner tends to be consistent with one of these types:

1. Relationship clients.

2. Fear-based clients.

3. Curious clients.

4. Greedy clients.

Relationship Clients

These people want to form a bond with someone whom they trust. They tend to be easy to talk to at the initial meeting. Much of the meeting time is conversational. Getting to know these clients as individuals is of utmost importance. They want to be comfortable. They tend to be very good long-term clients and very nice to work with. While they may defer to your recommendations, it is your responsibility to keep them involved in the process.

On the other hand, it is still important to establish boundaries and expectations with these clients. They need to understand how much communication from you will be provided in the relationship. You will like these clients and therefore unwittingly create unreasonable communication expectations by the length and frequency of your original phone calls. Also, don't shy away from communicating with these clients if something does not work as planned. The relationship could be quite hurt if you are too busy or too ashamed to call.

Also, since much of your meeting with a relationship client may be dealing with feelings and subjects other than wealth management, it is a good idea to summarize the business aspect of the meeting in a letter. This will help keep the business end of the relationship moving forward.

Fear-Based Clients

These people tend to have very little financial experience or have had bad financial experiences. Often they are the recent benefactors of an inheritance or the financially uninvolved spouse in a divorce, but they can also be busy professionals who are in control in all areas but money. These clients are also reliant upon you. They often need educating, although they may seemingly not want it. Your job is not to take care of them, but rather to work with them. You have to help them gain confidence in the money arena.

A frightened client may also defer to you, but you should make sure that he or she is not retreating from you. Things may seem overwhelming , so he or she may literally check out of the meeting. You may be talking and discover later that you were not really heard. You will want to keep the fear-based client involved and help him or her make decisions. Often these clients will procrastinate or abdicate and then just suddenly implement. The workplan will help you keep this client involved and active.

Here again, a summary letter outlining what you covered is important. It gives a reference point for the meeting and also helps foster confidence in the process. Most fear-based clients eventually become relationship or curious clients once their fears have been assuaged.

Curious Clients

German philosopher Walter Bennett stated, "All knowledge takes the form of interpretation." This is completely true of your knowledgeable clients. They are working with you because of time constraints. They take a great interest in what you do and will often imply that they would like to do what you do when they retire from their current profession. These clients will have formed their opinions through what they have read or heard. They often will continue to focus on items that validate their thinking.

You need to talk with these clients in great detail around issues that you may feel are fallacious. They are very good long-term clients if you are able to speak their language and provide enough support for what you are doing.

As these clients get to know you better, they may seem to become a relationship type of client. But don't underestimate their need for information and, ostensibly, control. After you have made decisions together, continue to support those decisions through articles that you find. Don't be afraid to readdress issues.

Greedy Clients

If someone has figured out how to work on a long-term basis with greedy clients, please write to me. These are often the clients who are only interested in some inarticulated and ever-changing objectives, usually measured by short-term results. They may appear to be charming initially because they are often marked by high energy and a quick mind. They are also often capricious. Unfortunately, they tend to initially put you on a pedestal and spend the rest of the relationship trying to knock you off it. These clients may come to you for planning, but are really concerned about returns, returns, returns.

These clients hate to lose. They obsess about their victories, kick themselves (or you) if something goes wrong, and are impossible to keep happy. I had a client who was furious with us for not having him fully invested in international funds one of the years they beat US stocks. In Roger Gibson's (the author of the seminal book on asset allocation) paradigm,[2] the greedy client would believe in market timing *and* stock selection.

I try not to work with these clients. Over time, they usually create havoc with your staff and force you to perform tasks that are unreasonable or unappreciated. Inevitably, they will also leave you.

Summary

All clients have qualities defined in each of the four categories, but their primary traits are normally easy to discern. With any one of these clients, you still need to appeal to the secondary characteristics as you concentrate on the primary ones. Getting to appreciate your clients' personalities is critical in developing a personal approach to their financial planning.

Also, it is highly likely when dealing with couples that each partner will have a different phenotype. This will test your flexibility, but you must relate to each spouse. Ultimately, a part-

---

[2] Roger C. Gibson, *Asset Allocation: Balancing Financial Risk* (Burr Ridge, IL: Irwin Professional Publishing, 1990).

nership profile is developed in which the dominant personality controls most of the decisions. Unfortunately, by dealing only with the partnership profile, you may be not securing the relationship with the more passive or introverted partner.

There are some other excellent tools to help you identify the type of clients with whom you may be dealing. Wilson Learning (based in Minneapolis) offers an excellent program in social styles. This program identifies the following four dominant traits of people and helps you classify people under one (or a combination) of them: analytical, amiable, driver, or expressive. Each personality type prefers to receive information differently and has different relationship needs.

The Meyers-Briggs psychological profile identifies 16 different quadrants based on how people process information and relate to each other: feeling or thinking, intuitive or sensing, perceiving or judging, and thinking or feeling. Trying to identify in which quadrant your clients currently reside will help you relate to them more effectively.

Also there are some excellent books written by financial professionals who have tremendous experience in working with the feelings people have about money. Kathleen Gurney,[3] Victoria Felton-Collins,[4] and Ruth Hayden[5] have all published meaningful work on this topic.

Fact Finding

Understanding the client is central to everything we do. It is so easy to become unclear. There is a story of a man whose father

---

[3] Kathleen Gurney, *Your Money Personality: How It Is and How You Can Profit from It* (New York, Doubleday, 1988).

[4] Victoria Felton-Collins, *Couples and Money: Why Money Interferes with Love and What to Do About It* (New York, Bantam, 1990).

[5] Ruth L. Hayden, *How to Turn Your Money Life Around: The Money Book for Women* (Deerfield Beach, FL: Health Communications, Inc., 1992).

died. He tells the undertaker that he wants to give Dad the very best. They have the funeral and the man gets a bill for $16,000. He pays it. A month later he gets a bill for $85, which he pays, and the next month he gets another $85 bill. Same thing the following month. Finally he calls the undertaker, who says, "Well, you said you wanted the best for your dad. So I rented him a tux."

After getting to know clients and developing an understanding of their predilections, you can then delve into the facts of their individual situations. This is typically done through a fact-finding form (see Appendix D for a copy of our form) and copies of all their statements. As you go through the assembled data, continue to ask clients why they own this or that, being very careful not to criticize or attack past decisions. You want to understand what motivations precipitated investment or consumer decisions. Ask them what they have liked and disliked about these decisions or about the people with whom they have worked previously. Don't assume that poor performance was the motivation behind seeking help.

You need to gather enough information to adequately assess the facts of the situation. The hurdle here is that the absence of the coordination of information may have brought the client to you in the first place. We try to make things as easy as possible. For those who have the details, we try to get them; for those who don't, we ask for statements and contacts so we may better gather the information ourselves.

Fact finding needs to be completely nonjudgmental. All of us make choices based on the outcomes for which we are either searching or avoiding. This typically means pursuing pleasure or avoiding pain. The consequences of our choices may not be predictable, yet the anticipated results are the catalyst for our actions. To sit in judgment after having the benefit of hindsight is not only unproductive, but it can also impact the depth with which the client will continue to take emotional risks and share information with you.

It is often easier for you to do the legwork in obtaining information for the client. Ask the client to bring in any available statements. In areas such as tax or estate planning, ask clients for signed permission to speak to their other advisors. It may cost them slightly more up front, but it will give you a good sense of why decisions were made regarding tools like trusts, powers of attorney, leasing versus buying, etc.

This also helps establish relationships with the other advisors so that checks and balances can be done away from the client, removing the deleterious impact of advisors challenging each other in front of the client and thereby damaging everyone's credibility, leaving the client confused and mistrustful.

Sometimes individual advisors do not have the fact patterns behind the decisions that are about to be made. It is much more useful for the client to have all the advisors in agreement on an approach. Alternative ideas should be presented with the consensus being articulated. The client ultimately always makes the choice on his or her own plan; if consensus among advisors is not reached in advance, that choice may be overwhelming.

One of the most difficult tasks in the fact-finding arena is attempting to understand our clients' feelings toward volatility. This is especially important, though, in the context of the other risks they choose to accept by rejecting volatility. Defining risk is a very difficult, almost insurmountable, task. At its most primitive level, it is a "sleep factor"—those results that would cause the client to lose sleep at night.

The 1980s was a period of extraordinary growth in the stock market, lulling many of us into a misunderstanding of our clients' risk tolerance. This is in part due to an inadvertent misguidance from them. If volatility is predominately upward, the perceived loss of gain becomes a greater risk to the client than the perceived loss of capital. Unfortunately, this perception is illusory. The challenge is to somehow move the client away from what is happening at the moment and to try to refocus on a range of possible outcomes.

The best way of doing this is through the forced choice. With forced choice decisions, you list, for instance, the characteristics that you want your investments to have. Four typical categories may be

1. Produce income.

2. Maintain principal.

3. Grow faster than inflation.

4. Provide tax advantages.

If you give your client nine points to spread among those four categories, the client begins to put a value on what he or she wants. The client also begins to realize that there is a relative value among investment choices; no individual investment does all things.

Assessing the client's feelings toward the trade-offs inherent in financial planning will help you create a meaningful financial plan. It will also help the client to create realistic expectations.

Baselining the Relationship

After you have spent adequate time finding out about the client, it's time to replay your understanding of his or her needs and wants through a letter. This letter outlines what you understand the client situation to be, what you will do for him or her, what the fee is, and how the relationship will work. It enables clients to assess how you understand them and to have good information with which to decide to engage you. We call this an engagement letter.

A well-crafted engagement letter will again focus on the client's needs and goals. More important, it is a critical first step in the process of managing expectations. A recitation of the facts is helpful primarily because it paints a clear picture of the obstacles that could impede the stated goals as well as assures the client that you heard and understand those goals. French/American writer Anaïs Nin said, "We don't see things as they are, we see them as we are." You must therefore go beyond the recitation of facts into some of the personal observations that the client shared with you regarding his or her money profile. As you again show clients that *you will be sensitive to who they are rather than just what they have,* you will create open and promising relationships.

The engagement letter is the first opportunity to get agreement on the way you each see things. The focus of the letter must be how you will help the client realize his or her dreams. Our firm's engagement letter is typically quite long (three to five pages).

We also tie what we will do for the client directly into the Wealth Management Index. We essentially outline the categories under an outline of our services and integrate that into the body of the engagement letter. By suggesting the areas that need to be covered in the same letter that outlines those areas that the client feels are most important, you have synthesized the client's expectations with yours.

It is quite easy to integrate the Wealth Management Index into the engagement letter. After outlining our understanding of the client's situation and what we have heard to be the client's key objectives, we then take each of the five Wealth Management Index categories and give a brief discussion of the client's shortcomings within the index. I have included a sample letter as Appendix A.

I want to make a case here for choosing your clients carefully. Do not work with everyone who wants to work with you.

You need to determine the value of the work that you are doing and be compensated fairly for that effort. You also want a relationship that will be mutually beneficial and enjoyable. Since our fees tend to start out at the higher end, we will often help people find planners who may work differently than we do and are therefore less expensive. Part of your job is determining whether you can offer value to match the cost of the service. If you can't, then you'd better walk away early. It took me a long time to learn this lesson, but it has made a tremendous difference in my practice.

Performing Analyses

Once you have been retained, you are free to start inputting the data into whatever computer programs you use that can give you balance sheets, cash flows, tax projections, and summary data. I believe that these programs are tremendously useful for diagnostic purposes within a relatively short time horizon.

I am not a believer in running projections out for the next 30 years. In fact, I almost think that this is tantamount to malpractice. Does anyone really believe that a retirement income projection performed for a 40-year-old who wants to retire in 20 years is any more reliable than predicting what the Dow will be then? Camus said, "Real generosity towards the future lies in giving all to the present." We need to meld our clients' short- and long-term objectives by maximizing all the decisions that are made today. We should be giving our clients a menu of choices, not dictating values. In many ways, the prognostications of the future are our value decisions softened by numbers.

I firmly believe that the client needs to grasp his or her situation today and see what it could look like over a maximum of 5 years. I also believe that we need to surface the question of the future in the context of evaluating all our goals. I am just not sold that projecting out 30 years is the best way of doing this.

Lynn Hopewell, a highly respected financial planner from Falls Church, Virginia, awakened me to the complexity of long-term projections through a Monte Carlo simulation he did at a meeting I attended. He took a routine subject like college planning, something we all do, and produced a Monte Carlo scattergram for it. By expanding the rate-of-return possibilities only slightly (1 percent on each side), and increasing or decreasing the inflation rate by one percent, the range of saving necessary to reach target was increased by 50 percent in each direction from the fixed point analysis that most of us do. Now add to that all the factors that should get thrown into long-term projections—taxes, government benefits, health considerations, job changes—and ask yourself whether you want the client to be clinging to your assumptions 10 years from now. Respect Camus, and at least give most to the present and maybe just a little bit to the near future.

We use a Monte Carlo simulation program called Crystal Ball in our practice. We find it very helpful in showing ranges of outcomes. As the client sees the range of possibilities for results, he or she is then able to determine the amount of risk acceptable in reaching his or her objectives. This is a significant shift away from how much risk the client would accept from an investment. The focus for clients becomes how they can accomplish what they set out to do; the Monte Carlo gives them a graphic picture of the obstacles.

As you share with clients their current situations and your 5-year analysis, you can begin to establish criteria for the Wealth Management Index. You are showing clients a snapshot of how things are right now and the effects of a "change nothing" approach over the next 5 years. All areas of the index are involved in this step, albeit some more discreetly than others. You should make them all surface and begin setting the benchmarks.

Some of the spreadsheets or financial planning tools would be better used by the clients themselves. For example, explore setting clients up on a personal finance program such as Quicken. Clients who like using the computer can handle input themselves. Those who are computer-wary could furnish their information to you (for a monthly service fee) and you would provide them with the printouts monthly. It may also be possible to have the clients use a bank that is tied into Quicken and a credit card that downloads information automatically into the program. This would enable you to have accurate client cash flow data whenever you need it.

Planning aspects would be integrated modularly (tax runs, needs analysis, etc.). In doing this, you are preemptively establishing your value on the advice side by recognizing that organizing data is a critical task but not one that requires great skill. With the love affair with do-it-yourself programs, this integrated client relationship recognizes what the client can do on their own and yet supports your unique skills in consulting.

There is a chance that clients are in position to meet all of their goals. Modeling lets clients see this. The "change nothing" approach can help you understand with them if what they expressed were truly their goals or were instead limits set by their expectations of achievement. Some people set their sights artificially low because they want to be sure they can reach them. Many people are so firmly planted in their reality that even when they are encouraged to dream, they are unable to break away from their self-imposed constraints.

Creating a Workplan

The workplan is created after you have set up the criteria for the Wealth Management Index against which you measure success. The workplan is your individual client flowchart that will go over everything from how many meetings you will have with the client, to how many telephone contacts, to any special considerations or interests. We even include a per-client marketing budget for things such as charity events to which we have been invited or wish to invite them to. The workplan is also how you will benchmark your success, and the communication of this success, toward the Wealth Management Index throughout the year.

As the years go by with your client, you should be able to produce a year-by-year journal of the successes that you have had. The nonsuccesses are addressed on next year's workplan. It is virtually impossible to fully accomplish all that you set out to do each year; it is important to carry forward those things left untended to help gauge next year's success. All successes are therefore captured in an annual running list; all nonsuccesses are appropriately dealt with through next year's workplan.

In order for the workplan to be effective, it is critical to have a task and contact system set up in your office. The recall system that you set up has to be effective for how you run your practice. There are many things that you can do, ranging from project programs, to database management, to a simple one-card filing system. Don't get bogged down in systems, pay attention to results.

Communicating with Clients

You cannot minimize the importance of client contact. We learned from Jim Budros and Peggy Ruhlin, who run a tremendously successful planning practice in Columbus, Ohio, the value of this seemingly obvious point. All of their client contact is planned and laid out in expectations established at the annual review.

The Wealth Management Index compels you to meet quarterly with your clients to be sure that you are on track with all the areas within the index. These quarterly meetings should have a set agenda; for example, you could focus one meeting on insurance and estate planning, one meeting on asset allocation, one meeting on cash flow and tax planning, and one meeting (annual review) on summarizing the year's progress and establishing next year's values. Each meeting should also have the unique elements of the client's plan that you agreed upon in your annual engagement letter. Contacts between these meetings will ensure that you are the primary source for their financial questions.

Summary

This client contact is expensive. High service planning means a limiting of clients to deliver the best possible planning. It also means charging appropriately for the delivery of this service. On the other hand, few people are receiving this intimate level of service. You can distinguish yourself quickly with this planned attentiveness.

All of this is really expectations management—the single most important component of retaining satisfied clients.

3

SCORING THE WEALTH MANAGEMENT INDEX

An article in the March 1996 *Atlantic Monthly* discussed medicine. It referred to the California medical board and how it seemed to be shrouded in secrecy regarding complaints. If you can disregard the secrecy involved with the complaint procedure, the article points out interesting aspects about where medicine has come from that are relevant to financial planning today:

> This secrecy is rooted in the past, when medicine was quasi-religious, and flourishes today, when it is quasi-scientific. . . . Medical secrecy is comprehensible as the almost instinctive attempt of the profession to cushion itself against its major hazard—error . . . it is perhaps the feeling that outsiders will never understand the full context of risk and contingency that makes colleagues so tight-lipped. . . . As professionals, doctors claim mastery over a field of esoterica, and patients must defer to their expertise. The professional motto [sociologist Everest] Hughes points out is not the businessman's *Caveat Emptor* but *Credat Emptor*—"Let the taker believe in us."[1]

---

[1] Judith Gingold, "Adventures in Liposuction," *Atlantic Monthly*, March 1996, p. 100.

As financial planners, we are weaned on modern portfolio theory and injected with ample doses of future projections and expected results. But these are only expectations. We represent a soft science and by definition our results are impossible to accurately predict. To the extent that our clients take certainty in the probabilities we espouse, we may be guilty of mismanaging expectations. The scoring of the Wealth Management Index is more than another attempt to quantify the unquantifiable; it is a way to work with your clients in their establishment of the range of results that we seek. Robert Arnott has defined risk as the "vulnerability of any undesirable consequences." This could be anything from volatility risk to what Arnott terms "maverick risk"—the risk of being different from the crowd.[2] The client/ planner partnership created through the scoring of the index will greatly aid you in addressing a client's feelings about the more obscure and often unidentified risks that he or she is unwilling to accept.

This client knowledge is the complete key to success in what we do. Warren Buffet tells a story about knowing the client:

> A fisherman goes into a sporting goods store to buy a lure. The sales clerk shows him a wide array of colored feathers, plastic insects, and other ingenious enticements for the fisherman to use. Trying to select a lure that will help him increase his chances, the fisherman asks, Do fish really like this sort of thing? To which the clerk answers, I don't sell to fish.

We need to develop a system of working with the client that enables us to use our vast portfolio of knowledge in a way that impresses not other planners but our clients. Our job is not to impart everything we know to the client, it is to bridge our knowledge with the client's desires to create a flexible and effec-

---

[2] Robert D. Arnott, *The Portable MBA in Investment*, ed. Peter L. Bernstein (New York: John Wiley & Sons, 1995), pp. 220–21.

tive financial plan. This can be done through the Wealth Management Index.

There may be some disagreement over the relative weighting of any particular category in the index, but I caution you against making any major changes in these categories. They have been carefully evaluated in the context of total success in reaching one's goals and dreams. They have been laid out without, for example, too much emphasis on the particular piece of my practice that I enjoy the most (asset management) and have been assembled to best help create a cogent, strategic, and inclusive financial plan.

The index was also created as much as possible away from the clutter of the things that most capture our imagination, like the daily gyrations of the stock market. It is set up to withstand the test of time and to aid our clients in enjoying their time. It strikes a balance between what the client wants tomorrow and what he or she wants today and places the client as the fulcrum.

Last, the index forces you as the planner to be more than just conversant on the many aspects of a well-crafted financial plan. Successfully using the index means keeping current with the changes that take place daily in our environment. Wealth management is comprehensive, complex, and compassionate. To effectively make this concept work you must be part economist, part psychologist, part investment manager, part minister, and have scores of other skills that help make our job so vibrant.

Components of the Wealth Management Index

The various components of the Wealth Management Index are explained throughout the book as they fall under the broad categories outlined in Chapter 1. I would like to take you through each individual component of the Wealth Management Index and help explain how to score them. The book itself will go into greater detail of the components. The actual numbers given, though, are jointly determined by you and the client.

I have listed these items in order of overall weighting for the index, not in the context of the index.

1. Is Your Asset Allocation Appropriate?   10%

The primary areas covered here are

- ◆ Development of a coherent investment philosophy.
- ◆ Determination of the investment policy.
- ◆ Rebalancing to the investment policy.

The development of a coherent investment philosophy is worth only 20 percent of this category because it will be made concrete in the investment policy. This is the regular discussion around issues such as risk tolerance as well as the decision regarding how much additional growth is needed to satisfy the objectives.

The written investment policy represents 60 percent of this area. You must first determine whether you are a strategic (passive) asset allocator or tactical (active) allocator. This will influence your crafting of the policy and the flexibility you allow within it. Points would be subtracted for deviation from the policy. It is possible to have enhanced performance in a given year through ignoring the policy and overemphasizing particular investments, but this would not be rewarded within the discipline of the Wealth Management Index.

Even for the strategic asset allocator, after a particularly strong string of returns, the question must be broached as to whether the original allocation is acceptable. This brings up the issues around utility of returns discussed in Chapter 6. It may involve changing the policy to reflect the need for greater or lesser returns based on the distance from the client's stated objectives.

You also must have defined your rebalancing parameters with the client in the investment policy. To score this area involves the actual rebalancing of the portfolio as well as the decisions around the portfolio allocation. This represents 20 percent of the section. The rebalancing parameters should be laid out in the investment policy and implemented accordingly.

2. Were Your Annual Contributions or Withdrawals at Target?   10%

This portion of the Wealth Management Index involves dollars withdrawn or contributed to the portfolio in accordance with the investment policy.

The management of the client portfolio is dependent on the flow of money in or out of the plan. The time-weighted returns used to measure performance for AIMR standards are less functional for financial planners who have so much control over the timing of investments. Withdrawing more money than planned or not contributing at an expected level has tremendous impact on the success of the allocation strategies.

When scoring this area, a perfect score would be contributing or withdrawing at the expected level, contributing more than expected, or withdrawing less than expected. If the client exceeds expected withdrawals or does not reach intended investment levels, then the score would be reduced accordingly. While there may be good reason for not reaching the objectives, the client is still adversely impacted by missing targets. We tend to give zero scores only in cases in which the client dramatically missed the plan. Partial scores can be awarded for achieving certain savings levels, but not at the intended level.

3. Are Your Business Interests Adequately Covered?   8.5%

The four key areas for determining the adequacy of business interests are to

- Verify appropriate business form.
- Perform valuation.
- Establish keep/sell agreements.
- Fund for death and disability.

While not all clients will have businesses with which this area is of concern, for those who do have businesses (and, as explained in Chapter 4, some clients have businesses of which they are completely unaware), this piece of the Wealth Management Index is very important. In scoring this area, we would give the most importance to business form, because the success of the enterprise is greatly influenced by the chosen operating entity. Place up to a third of the points on form.

Place 50 percent of the points on establishing keep/sells (and reviewing them) as well as funding them. Points are to be awarded for the decision with regard to the funding. It may be completely appropriate to choose to fund from cash flow, as long as this is by design rather than by default; credit the maximum amount of points here.

Roughly 17 percent of the points in this section involve valuing the business and regularly reviewing this valuation. Valuation procedures are often spelled out in the keep/sell documents, but they are also not often referred to. The valuation plays a significant role in estate planning as well as income planning.

We give full points to someone who doesn't have business interests. I caution you, though. It is amazing how many people have these interests but don't classify them as such.

4. Do You Have an Appropriate Amount of Life Insurance, Consistent with an Articulated Philosophy Around This Insurance?   8.25%

The decisions around the ownership of life insurance are complex. Scoring within this Wealth Management Index component involves

- ◆ Determining the level of the client's desire to provide adequate support for his or her partner should he or she die first.
- ◆ Developing a firm understanding of the client's assets and creating a sense of comfort with projected assets.
- ◆ Allowing the client to choose the level of estate taxes that his or her heirs will have to pay.

Most of the value of this area is determined by the discussions in setting up a life insurance philosophy and then making sure the philosophy is implemented. Forty-five percent of this area is for the development of the philosophy and 45 percent is for the implementation.

The final 10 percent is the estate tax analysis. It represents such a minor component because if estate taxes are a huge current concern, they would be detailed and provided for through the establishment of the philosophy. If the client is relatively young and not as concerned about projecting estate taxes 30 or 40 years out, then the discussion and decision about taxes still needs to happen, but it does not have to be overemphasized.

5. Have You Protected Yourself Against Catastrophic Loss Due to Long-Term Care, Property Losses, or Liability Issues?   8.25%

Catastrophic planning is covered in detail in Chapter 4, but the most important thing about it is that it is easy for clients to protect themselves from catastrophes. This portion of the Wealth Management Index centers on

- ◆ Dictating the parameters around property/casualty insurance purchases.
- ◆ Making decisions regarding long-term care.
- ◆ Deciding on whether asset transference or retitling is appropriate for liability reasons or long-term care concerns.

Since property/casualty insurance can cover most of the most likely potential calamities in this area of the Wealth Management Index, the property/casualty analysis is worth 50 percent of the points here. Clients need to understand that this insurance is not a necessary evil but a tremendous way to decide between self-insuring risk or passing it off to the insurance company.

The long-term care decision is worth 25 percent of the points because providing long-term care could not only cause tremendous financial hardship on a client, but the discussion also affords you the opportunity to better understand what the client's longevity and lifestyle concerns are. This discussion cuts across this area and into the estate planning side as well.

Twenty-five percent is also attributed to asset transference because it needs to be regularly discussed and implemented often well in advance of any potential problems. Transference can be as simple as retitling of assets to as complex as offshore trusts. Pragmatism must prevail over planning here, as explained in Chapter 4.

6. Does Your Will Match Your Wealth Transfer Wishes?   8%

For many of our clients, leaving a legacy is one of their ultimate goals. This area of the Wealth Management Index focuses on the following items for scoring purposes:

- Establishment of objectives for the estate plan.
- Drafting of the necessary documents.

Understanding your client's desires around wealth transfer is what will drive the document that ultimately disposes of the estate. Unfortunately, if the actual will has not been drawn, then the state in which the client lives has drafted one for them. This is why the detailed outline of the client's objectives is worth 30 percent of this area and the actual drafting of the will (and any other necessary documents) represents 70 percent.

While the wishes of the client may not change annually, the planner should still affirm those wishes in a review each year.

7. Do You Have Too Much or Too Little Disability Protection Given Your Assets and Income and Will the Coverage Pay You Should You Be Unable to Work?   8%

As you work with your clients throughout the years, you will be placing them in a position of financial independence. The disability planning area of the Wealth Management Index is multidimensional and points are garnered for

- Assessment of the income needs of the client in case of his or her inability to work.
- Discussion of the value of self-funding, if appropriate.
- Implementation or self-insuring.

This area needs to be regularly reviewed because as clients' assets increase, their predilection toward self-funding may increase. We value the needs assessment and the implementation decision as equally important and give 90 percent of the scoring to those two areas.

While the discussion of self-funding is necessary, it represents only 10 percent because it is ultimately contained in the implementation framework. The client may choose to self-fund because of insurance costs even though he or she is ill-prepared to do it. Should this be the case, points would still need to be deducted from the index because acceptance of risk is appropriate only if the probability of occurrence is judged to be extremely small or if the cost to protect is prohibitive. While costs to protect with disability coverage may seem expensive to the client, they are usually not prohibitive (severely rated cases may be the exception).

We always allocate points for the discussion around a topic. It is through these discussions that you and the client will either reach a mutually agreeable decision or come upon an impasse that may not make working together feasible. With either result, both you and the client are ultimately better off.

8. Are Your Assets Titled Correctly and Have You Set Up Appropriate Beneficiary Designations? 5%

This 5 percent could be extremely costly if not regularly reviewed, updated, and recorded. Scoring involves

- Insuring that all assets with which a beneficiary designation is allowed have the correct one.
- Evaluating what types of retirement accounts need to be established, split, or used for charitable purposes.
- Reviewing ownership of assets.

This area is highly complex and can help your clients to retain the greatest amount possible of their assets while meeting their wealth transfer wishes. We view all 3 areas as equally important and they should be reviewed annually. Points need to be awarded for the surfacing of the issues as well as the implementation of the solutions. While it is true that there may be very few necessary changes from year to year, the area still needs to be closely reviewed.

Also, this part of the Wealth Management Index considers the client's ultimate death and the decisions the beneficiaries must make with regard to decedent IRAs or withdrawal issues. In the year that this occurs, this may be the single most important decision you can ever make with your client.

9. Did You Receive in Income (Earnings, Gifts, Social Security, Pension) What You Expected to This Year?   4%

This piece represents the first half of the cash flow portion of the Wealth Management Index. While it may be somewhat difficult to control this area, it is imperative that we understand it. This is done through

- ◆ Discussing what will be expected in income this year and the timing of this income.
- ◆ Establishing items with which the client may exert some timing discretion.
- ◆ Insuring that the client applies for all benefits to which he or she is entitled.

Understanding what can be expected this year and when it may come is worth 60 percent of this piece. The client is penalized for overly optimistic assumptions because these are typically used to drive many other aspects of the plan, including the investment policy. The client is not necessarily rewarded for better income numbers because we are most concerned with accuracy in forecasting. The better income numbers are nice, but they were not on what the plan was established.

Timing issues can often be managed, particularly with spending policies on investment accounts and income deferral decisions. The timing decision is often integrated with tax projections to try to derive the greatest benefit to the client. We value these timing issues as 30 percent of this category.

Application for all possible benefits represents only 10 percent of the category but it can be easily overlooked. This is especially true for clients who may have worked in other countries. Full points are rewarded for exploring this area.

10. Did You Use All Reasonable Means to Reduce Your Taxes? 4%

A thorough understanding of the client's present and potential future tax situation is reviewed and scored in this section. This would include

- Preparing a tax estimate and determining the marginal federal tax bracket and any benefits of straddling between tax years.
- Reviewing and implementing all appropriate tax minimization strategies ranging from retirement plans (including deferred comp) to full use of cafeteria plans to insuring interest deductions.
- Planning around stock options.
- Evaluating charitable planning, asset transference, and investment tax minimization.

Understanding the client's marginal tax rate is the foundation for any type of tax planning. For scoring purposes, this receives 30 percent of the Wealth Management Index points.

How the client uses this information to effect change by implementing tax minimization programs is arguably as important and also receives 30 percent of the points. Points would be deducted if the client chose not to fully participate in company-sponsored tax-advantaged retirement plans with his or her first dollars earmarked toward retirement planning.

Stock-option planning for corporate clients represents 20 percent of the points available. Decisions to defer or introduce option income (in an attempt to convert ordinary income to long-term capital gains) for clients with nonqualified stock options make this essential not only to cash flow planning but also to tax planning. Alternative minimum tax considerations with incentive stock options also create important tax ramifications. While the decision to defer options or exercise them may be somewhat arbitrary, the discussion around the decision is how points need to be credited.

Any asset transference strategies total the final 20 percent of this tax planning component. Since asset transference often involves irrevocable decisions, again the assessment of the alternatives involved and the conscious choice of rejecting or accepting asset transference determines the Wealth Management Index point total.

11. Did You Spend According to Plan?   4%

How clients spend their money represents 4 percent of the Wealth Management Index. This area, as described in Chapter 5, constitutes the values not necessarily verbally expressed by the client, but rather acted upon by him or her. Developing an appropriate cash flow model and managing back to this model will enable the clients to score all the available points here. Maximum points are given for spending according to plan; if the client foregoes a planned vacation, he or she doesn't get extra credit. Clients set up their cash flow with you in an environment that encourages them to express their spending wishes. If they don't spend according to those wishes, then their actions do not reflect their words.

12. Is Your Current Ratio Better than 2:1 and Is Your Total Debt Reasonable as a Percentage of Your Assets? 4%

Almost everyone who enters our offices states their major objective for financial planning as freedom to do what they want to do when they want to do it. Inappropriate debt may represent the greatest barrier to this freedom. Bulwer Lytton, writing in *Caxtoniana* in 1864, says: [The inappropriate use of] "Debt is to man what the serpent is to the bird; its eye fascinates, its breath poisons, its coil crushes sinew and bone, its jaw is the pitiless grave."[3]

The Wealth Management Index explores and scores both short-term and overall debt. It involves

- Understanding the financial planning current ratio as outlined in Chapter 6.

- Determining how debt can be used effectively rather than oppressively.

If the current ratio is better than 2:1, then the client gets 50 percent of the available points here. For ratios worse than that, points are deducted. Any client with more short-term debt than assets would get zero points on this section of the index.

Overall debt also needs to be reviewed for the final 50 percent here. Determining the reasonableness of the debt level needs to be done in conjunction with the client. For example, a client who has a very predictable income stream may be comfortable with much larger amounts of debt than a client whose income is unpredictable. While Chapter 6 describes ratios that may be helpful in general, comfort around debt is very personal and needs to evaluated accordingly.

---

[3] Bulwer Lytton, "Caxtoniana," in *The Oxford Book of Money*, ed. Kevin Jackson (Oxford: Oxford University Press, 1995), p. 215.

13. Have You Established and Funded All Necessary Trusts?   3%

The number of clients that have come into our offices with wonderfully intricate yet unfunded trusts amazes me. An unfunded revocable living trust is truly the emperor without clothes. Therefore, in scoring your Wealth Management Index clients:

- Explore the use of trusts as a financial planning tool.
- Establish those trusts deemed appropriate.
- Maximize the funding of the trusts that require it.

Not all clients require trusts, but virtually all clients need to discuss the possibilities of using them. Trusts may be as simple as Uniform Transfer to Minor's Accounts (UTMAs) to as complex as offshore asset-protection trusts. The discussion around trusts in general is worth a third of this area.

Clients may agree that trusts would be a good idea and then never get around to setting them up. Developing and instituting these vehicles represents another one-third of the points in this area.

Once clients have set up the trusts with which they are comfortable, they may need to place assets in them. Since certain trusts have annual funding limitations and other trusts may be somewhat ineffective without being fully funded, asset transference must be discussed and potentially implemented annually.

14. Do You Need and Have a Power of Attorney, a Health Care Declaration, or a Living Will?   3%

The best plans may be rendered ineffective because proper advance planning around emotional issues like power of attorney and health care declarations have not been set up or communicated. Here, the Wealth Management Index score comes from

◆ Discussing the aspects of decision-making powers in case of incapacitation, life support concerns, and any other final wishes.

◆ Establishing written procedures to enable the family to execute those wishes.

Chapter 8 goes through the thought process involved in this emotionally charged area. We score our Wealth Management Index clients equally between coming to agreement on the issues mentioned and then having appropriate paperwork drafted and signed.

As the client candidly talks about this area, it will also give you tremendous insight into other important estate transference issues. For example, the durable power of attorney discussion will encourage clients to discuss whom they trust with decision-making authority and will underscore control issues they may have.

15. Have You Access to as Much Debt as Reasonably Possible and at the Best Available Rates?   3%

I was sitting in a meeting with a group of bankers and one of my clients as we were trying to obtain financing for a project the client developed. This was a relatively new retail concept, so drawing on comparables was difficult. The client had prepared an extremely attractive memorandum with quite modest assumptions. One of the bankers said, "If you had a 2-year operating history with these numbers we would be happy to finance your transaction." I responded, "I appreciate your willingness to lend my client money at the time he is least inclined to need it."

We view establishing extensive credit as a fundamental tool in financial planning. While Chapter 6 discusses this area in detail, availing clients to credit enables them to potentially avoid the interaction I described above. For scoring, the two key areas are

- Exploring all avenues to qualify for free credit.
- Intensely negotiating the rates and covenants on this credit.

Obtaining (but not necessarily utilizing) the most free credit possible for the client is worth 70 percent of the points here. Credit should include everything from home equity loans, business loans, credit card lines, and personal lines. The purpose is to have the credit available; it is not to use it.

Negotiating the rates and guarantees or covenants on this credit represents 30 percent of the index. Each year, clients should try to improve on the lending rates and also try to have personal guarantees released. Scoring is for the negotiation, it is not for the ultimate result. It may not be possible to have a guarantee lifted, but the client should be working with you to try to get relief from the guarantees or from joint and several obligations.

16. How Did Your Actual Rate of Return Compare with the Expected Rate (CPI Plus Target Percentage)?   2.5%

In the investment policy discussed in Chapter 7, the rate-of-return benchmark that you set with the client is the CPI plus some percent. For growth-oriented portfolios it may be plus 6 or 7 percent; for balanced portfolios it may be plus 4 to 5 percent.

This brings to focus that the yardstick for measuring the ongoing wealth of the client is the CPI. Returns that trail inflation after taxes will most likely result in the client not meeting his or her objectives. To benchmark asset-allocated portfolios against the S&P 500 is not only unfair, but it is also off point. In periods of tremendous returns for international stocks, the fact that your client beat the returns of 500 US stocks is like comparing the 200 meter times of Jesse Owens who ran the distance to Mark Spitz who swam it. The information may appear interesting, but it is useless.

For scoring the Wealth Management Index, we compare against the CPI plus our agreed-upon percentage return. If we match or exceed that, then full points are credited. We reduce the points by the percentage off this benchmark. For example, if we are trying to achieve CPI plus 6 percent and we end up at CPI plus 4 percent, we reduce our point total by one-third. We score zero points in any year that we trail the CPI.

17. Have You Managed Your Debt as Expected? 2%

The Wealth Management Index covers not only how your debt is structured, but also how it is utilized. Planning to borrow is an acceptable financial planning alternative. Borrowing more than planned is not. You establish with the client what the anticipated use of borrowing will be for the year. In this category, scoring is all or nothing. If the client only borrowed what he or she had intended, the maximum score is given; if the client borrowed any more than anticipated, then he or she gets no points.

18. Have You Set Aside Enough Cash for Purchases to Be Made in the Next 3 Years? 1.25%

This piece of the index is covered in two components:

- ◆ Evaluating all cash needs in the next 3 years.
- ◆ Raising cash in advance of these needs.

Every year, we need to sit with our clients and determine what short-term expectations or desires they have. This discussion is of paramount importance for cash flow planning, investment purposes, and gifting strategies.

The scoring for the Wealth Management Index reflects 60 percent of the points here for forecasting what cash requirements will be needed for the client. The discussion is prospective; scoring is retrospective. If the client's cash requirements were greater than anticipated, zero points are awarded. We are trying to help the clients accept their own decisions about purchases and be accountable for them.

The rest of this piece of the Wealth Management Index is for the actual setting aside of the cash to reflect these anticipated purchases. Clients may choose to dedicate their declared bonuses for these items, but anticipated bonuses must be discounted for planning purposes. Also, using stock options may be a way to finance these purchases, but this does not preclude the need to set aside the cash anyway.

We had a client pair who was going to use their options for part of the down payment on a house they were planning to build in the next 2 years. The value of their stock options had dropped dramatically just as they were finalizing the plans with the architect. Since we were counting on the exercise of these options to reduce our mortgage costs, we were faced with either exercising many more options than we had originally planned (foregoing a tremendous amount of opportunity costs) or radically changing the structure of the mortgage. If we had been exercising options well in advance of the building, this would not have been a problem. We made the mistake of letting the potential of the stock cloud our judgment in developing our cash strategy.

Scoring this 40 percent then is the act of setting the money aside. Full points are awarded for having all money in place well in advance of the purchases.

19. Was the Portfolio Income Tax Efficient? 1.25%

This is an area where pragmatism rules. Once you have determined with the client the desired asset allocation, you then need to work with him or her to decide which assets should be held in which type of accounts. Before year end, you also want to determine if there is any tax loss selling you may want to utilize. Points are awarded here for discussing with the client the alternatives and deciding together what would make the client most comfortable.

20. Is Your Debt Tax Efficient? 1%

Each year, as you evaluate all of the client's sources of debt, you need to attempt to make as much of this debt tax deductible as realistic. Full points are given here for going through the tracing issues discussed in Chapter 6 and changing what is appropriate.

21. Have You Made Your Desired Gifts for This Year? 1%

This yes-or-no question, discussed before year end (and preferably prior to December so the option to gift appreciated stock is still available), is all or nothing for points earned.

Tips on Scoring the Wealth Management Index

The easiest way to score the Wealth Management Index is to break it down into its component pieces and those pieces within each component (subcomponents), score each piece separately on a 10-point scale, and multiply the result against the overall component weight. If you add this score and multiply against the overall index percentage, you then get a raw overall component score. Multiply this by 10. Adding these individual raw score numbers will give your total Wealth Management Index score.

Here is the formula:

$$\{ [(\%C \times c1) + (\%C \times c2) + (\%C \times c \ldots)]C\} \times 10,$$

where

C	=	Component of Wealth Management Index (i.e., "Is your asset allocation appropriate" is 10%)
%C	=	Percent that the subcomponent represents of C (i.e., "Developing a coherent investment philosophy" is 60%)
c1 ... c ...	=	Points given on the subcomponent

For example, "Is your asset allocation appropriate?" represents 10 percent of the total Wealth Management Index score. This is comprised of three key components:

1. Development of a coherent investment philosophy, 20%.

2. Determination of the investment policy, 60%.

3. Rebalancing to the investment policy, 20%.

If you determined with the client that you have developed an investment philosophy that cannot only be understood, but can also be articulated, the client would receive 10 points. You would then multiply this against the 20 percent weighting for the "developing a coherent investment philosophy" piece. This would give a total of 2 points toward the "Is your asset allocation appropriate?" Wealth Management Index section.

If you laid out an investment policy that the client chose not to follow because he or she did not want to sell some individual stocks owned or because of market timing decisions, you would reduce the score in this part by an appropriate amount. For example, if someone refused to rid him- or herself of the company stock owned and this caused a 20 percent deviation in the large stock area (which probably must be rectified in the small or international stock area), you would reduce the total available points from 10 to 5 (or another agreed-upon number). This would give 3 points total to add to the score (5 points × 60% of the "Is your asset allocation appropriate?" category).

Finally, if you rebalance with the client according to plan, the client would score 10 points. When this is multiplied by the 20 percent credit here, a total of 2 absolute points are acquired.

Adding the three component sections, therefore, would result in a total point score of 7 points. When you multiply this by the 10 percent that this category accounts for, you get .7. Multiplying this by 10 will give you your 7 points. If this category was only worth 3 percent of the index, then your total point score would be 2.1.

When you have finished the scoring of the index for the client, you can then discuss the areas where improvement is needed to better the score for next year. As you can see, the scoring of the Wealth Management Index is a joint activity because you and the client set the objectives. The scoring is also relatively balanced among areas, reflecting that *total* wealth management is far more important than any single component of wealth management:

85–100   Financial plan should meet your objectives.

65–84   Financial plan needs to be more focused on your needs.

Under 65   Planning overhaul is necessary.

The scoring is relatively tight here. Eighty-five percent of the points on the Wealth Management Index is an excellent score and one that few people walking in off the street will have achieved. In fact, it may take more than 1 or 2 years to reach that level. The beauty of the Wealth Management Index, though, is that once that level has been attained, and if you continue to meet regularly with your client and make necessary adjustments, you can rest assured that strong scoring can be maintained.

4

ASSET PROTECTION (PRESERVATION)

This category is weighted fairly high relative to its peers for a very important reason: You don't get a second chance here. A bad year or even a bad investment can cause some major discomfort, but still, poor investment performance is not debilitating. Inadequate protection of assets, though, is unrecoverable. Interestingly, it is often an area where clients know they need work but, because of preconceived notions, they may be disinclined to spend sufficient time here. Almost no one likes thinking about death, business breakups, or lawsuits, so ample planning may not be given.

Asset protection is simply figuring a way to keep what you have. There are numerous planning alternatives in this area. Isolated, any single idea may seem absurd, but woven into the fabric of the plan, it may become reasonable. For example, why would any reasonable couple place all their investments in one spouse's name and all of their business interests in the other's? If the buy/sell document precludes spouses from an ownership position in the company, then this type of asset ownership may exist. Working through the index and workplan will lead to appropriate, integrated solutions here.

Percent of Index (25%) for Asset Protection (Preservation)

	Percent of Asset Protection Scale	Total Index Weight
Do you have an appropriate amount of life insurance, consistent with an articulated philosophy around this insurance?	33%	8.25%
Have you protected yourself against catastrophic loss due to long-term care, property losses, or liability issues?	33%	8.25
Are your business interests adequately covered?	34%	8.50

As we go through the components of asset protection, you will discover how intricate this piece of planning is and how integral it is to a successful financial future.

Do You Have an Appropriate Amount of Life Insurance, Consistent with an Articulated Philosophy Around That Insurance?

The development of a life insurance philosophy starts with the question, "Do you wish to provide adequate support for someone when you die?" To me, this means that if there is not a someone, why own life insurance? In some situations you could conceivably choose to own a policy to lock in coverage when you are healthy just in case you find someone you wish to support. This should not be the default position. The reasonableness test to wealth management involves reviewing family health issues with the client and making a joint decision to either accept this future insurability risk or to download it to the insurance company.

If you do choose to download this risk, you should almost certainly do so with term insurance and with a strong company that provides a convertibility feature. If the client is healthy, you continue to shop the term insurance. If the client is uninsurable, you convert the term into a cash value policy within the same company.

If support is the litmus test, then this obviously precludes owning life insurance on children. If the fundamental question is for whom does the client wish to provide some support, children owning insurance for their parents' benefit is superfluous.

Buying insurance now because it costs less, even though the client has no one for whom to provide, also seems imprudent. I don't often buy items that I don't need even though they are on sale. What is the cost of owning a solution for a problem that may never exist?

If the client does not wish to provide adequate support to anyone, then he or she doesn't need to worry about the life insurance decision at all. In this case, the conscious choice to decline providing support would maximize their total score in this area on the index. Although in most situations this is a terrible choice, it is one that our clients' need to make after fairly assessing the consequences. Our job is to outline both the *social* and *financial* costs associated with the decision, but it is not to make that decision for the client.

The scoring for the index must be client centered. Therefore, in evaluating the scoring for the life insurance component, the discussion around the philosophy is almost as important as the ultimate decision whether to insure. The discussion does not focus on the benefits of a product but on the results of the choice the client makes regarding protection for his or her family.

The dialogue aspect of our job is so important to the design results that to focus on the product component before fully understanding and agreeing on the objectives of the client will create a result that can work only through happenstance. This will cause confusion later. This is especially true with those clients who have a contempt for life insurance. If the issues are openly discussed, then you have a better chance of debasing the preconceived notions which create impediments to a successful financial plan.

If the client is making decisions which you find incredible or reprehensible, you need to evaluate whether you are doing a service by working with the client. Even though the choices made are the client's choices, in some situations it does not make sense to have a relationship with someone who chooses things that are an anathema to you. You are far better off severing the relationship early and refunding your fees than continually compromising your values. This can happen if you are primarily interacting with one member of a couple and he or she wants to make decisions that adversely affect the spouse. If your fee agreement is with the couple, then your obligation is to the couple.

If the client wishes to provide adequate support, then a capital needs analysis should be completed. A capital needs analysis is simply the present value of all of our future dreams. Unfortunately, the ease with which this is described is in direct contrast to how it is calculated.

First we need to look at what those dreams may be. The most typical is that clients want their partner to continue in the same lifestyle should one of them die, but many younger clients don't feel a need to provide this support forever.

The social or emotional "cost" question is how long they wish to render the support. The questions around this need to involve both partners so that realistic expectations can be determined. It is also important not to have the client equate a cost with this decision until you have ferreted out what the dream is. Preoccupation with costs inhibits the objectives. It is difficult to get to the heart of a client's goals when he or she is preoccupied with costs.

Once survivor lifestyle is explored, the next step is understanding all components of that lifestyle. A relatively simple question regards debt paydown. Many clients feel a strong need to have debts paid off when they die. The critical question is why. In most cases, what the client is referring to is the concept of security—a paid-off home, no outside loans, a chicken in the kettle, and two cars in the garage.

Security is malleable, though. It means different things to us at different times. It is better to find out what worries would be created by an unexpected death. As these worries are laid out, you can then tie them back into your plan through the Wealth Management Index. Debt paydown concerns can be a symptom of the broader issue of fear; uncovering and assuaging the fear is our role.

What other concerns do clients have beyond current lifestyle and debt? Most clients have issues regarding paying for their children's college education, retirement, future purchases, and shared dreams beyond lifestyle that the survivor may still wish to realize.

Everything to this point measures the living desires of the client. These are by definition temporary. The desires are temporary because under actuarial circumstances, the client will experience all these things while he or she is living and (at least until cryogenics is mastered) life is temporary. This also means that for the client who experiences successful financial planning, his or her assets will pay for all these opportunities as they arise.

Somehow, we have to put a value today on what these future desires cost. By doing so, we can then determine whether the client's assets today can pay for tomorrow's dreams. The most useful tool for this is a death capital needs analysis (DCNA).

I believe that when people die they come upon two doors. One says "Heaven" and the other says "Lecture on Heaven." The financial planners are lined up outside the "Lecture on Heaven" door. The DCNA is supposed to provide comfort to the clients that you are not going by the seat of the pants when you estimate the present value of their dreams. If you were able to determine how long a client will live, what college will cost when the children are ready to attend, what the tax rate will be as money is withdrawn from retirement plans, what inflation will average over his or her life expectancy, what the surviving spouse will earn during the remaining working years, what social security will look like during retirement, how much he or she stands to inherit and when it will be received, as well as countless other issues, then you would have an exact figure of the assets needed today to meet those dreams. Realistically, one must be somewhat flexible here.

A capital needs analysis is a useful tool for estimating the present value of the dreams, but it really does not have great predictive value. The analysis is a launching pad for a reasonable guess, but, here again, a well-structured Monte Carlo simulation will show you the wide range of results that are possible.

It is far more important to look regularly at those dreams to see what major changes have occurred. Each year the client lives, the analysis is more useful because it spans a shorter time period. If the analysis is recognized as dynamic rather than static, it is a much better tool.

In doing the analysis, have the client determine with you what assumptions to use for the components of the analysis. The client will then be making value decisions with regard to items like Social Security and rate-of-return expectations. This is important because the numbers on these analyses are often imposing. With an understanding of the input, consensus on the output is more likely. If you add the dimension of the Monte Carlo analysis, you are then letting the client choose what assumption risks *he or she* wishes to take.

If the client was forthcoming with his or her desires and you developed a strong DCNA simulation, you now have an objective number around which you can make some decisions. If the client has enough assets to meet this number, your work is done here until next year. If the client doesn't, then he or she needs to make some decisions regarding whether to ignore the shortfall or how to meet it. This is the life insurance issue.

Since these needs are by definition temporary, on the surface term insurance would make the most sense as a funding vehicle. But more important than the temporary aspect of the needs is the fluidity of them. Each year the client lives, the survivor should need less money because his or her assets may have grown and there is 1 year less of untimely death to support. If the client desires have not changed and you hit your assumption numbers, then you should have a pretty good sense of how much insurance can be dropped annually.

The insurance industry has changed dramatically since I have been in financial planning. Term insurance costs are getting more and more competitive. The insurance companies have securitized their products by offering variable life. Commissions have dropped precipitously, which should ultimately lead to an enhancement of cash values. The flexibility of that new product "universal life" has been both ballyhooed and booed. Niche products have been created to cater to special situations.

With all the excitement in the industry, the simple conclusion that we have drawn at Accredited Investors, Inc., is that you almost invariably need to fund temporary needs of 10 years or less with term insurance; needs longer than that with some form of low cost, strong performing cash value policy; and special needs (i.e., estate planning) with a special need policy. Given the dynamic nature of the DCNA, a flexible policy like universal or adjustable life (although costs may be slightly higher) is usually most appropriate for the interim need category.

The evaluation of which type of life insurance is most suitable starts with the underlying premise that once you have made a decision on the types of products, you then have to make a second decision on the companies involved. Especially with cash value products, we have a very strong bias toward companies that have long track records and strong management. We all know that there are several services that rate the past performance of companies and try to estimate a company's solvency.

Past performance of insurance companies can be somewhat compared to past performance of mutual funds. While the information that you obtain is important, it is not necessarily prescient. A planner must have a strong understanding of the investment policies, managers, and business prospects of the companies that they choose to represent.

One of the most expensive things that a client can do is change a cash value life insurance policy. As low- or no-load life insurance improves, this expense may be more benign, but in most instances a client should view a cash value choice as a permanent one. The planner has a responsibility to provide a thorough screen.

Just as there is no best mutual fund, there is no best insurance product or company. Clients (and planners) are on a never-ending quest for the insurance product that will always hold up under intense scrutiny and back-testing. There are several strong companies that will perform well. Managing your clients' expectations is letting them know upfront of several of the companies that you feel are excellent. If clients choose any of these, they will probably not be hurt.

Once the selection of companies has been made, the companies must be monitored. Things can change with companies and policies. If they are not performing up to expectations, you need to evaluate the cause immediately. You need to judge whether it is a reason that is affecting all companies or just the company in which your client has money.

For example, universal life insurance was the panacea of the 1980s. People were superfunding their policies and expecting that in a short time they could stop paying premiums. Unfortunately, as interest rates fell, the length of time for premium payments increased. To switch a client out of one of these policies into another one because of a cyclical change in the industry is preposterous.

On the other hand, some companies had rapidly deteriorating financial situations that potentially may have been recognized through thorough due diligence (I say potentially because sometimes things deteriorated so rapidly that you couldn't get out in time). In this situation, even though a switch would be costly, it would still have been appropriate. The Wealth Management Index forces you to review this annually, rather than solely at the point of implementation. Each year, this becomes a discussion item for evaluating your success in this part of the index. Modifications are made as you reanalyze the client results.

The Wealth Management Index measures the coherence of the philosophy around life insurance. While the DCNA represents the first component, a second part of that philosophy involves the estate tax issue. As I said earlier, the desire issue is temporary. If the client lives long enough and is successful in planning, assets will fund these wants. The estate tax issue comes into play when the client has accumulated so many assets that he or she will be able to pass them on upon death. This could create an entirely different type of life insurance need.

While the Wealth Management Index has an area under estate planning which will be discussed later in this book, the development of an insurance philosophy still involves estate tax concerns. If a client's assets are sufficient to provide the lifetime support necessary for heirs, then the obvious question is whether the assets are so large that an estate tax problem may exist. If the client is concerned about this, then you begin the estate plan.

The result of a thorough estate plan will be either the choice to accept the tax consequences of a large estate or the implementation of appropriate strategies to minimize this cost. If there still looks to be an estate tax liability that the client will need to pay, then he or she must make a choice regarding whether the heirs will bear the cost out of the assets of the estate or whether the costs will be handled presently through the purchase of life insurance.

In the most simple terms, properly structured life insurance can provide a cash infusion into the estate that is both income and estate tax free. This infusion will prevent the estate from spending its liquid assets to pay estate taxes.

There are current costs for this benefit. Structural costs are the costs involved in setting up the insurance in appropriate trusts; functional costs are the costs of the insurance itself. Cash value life insurance does provide a form of leverage since the premiums paid into the policy will never be greater than the face amount of the policy. If the policy is to be paid upon death, then this inevitable gain makes the benefits of owning the insurance extremely powerful. Essentially, you would compare the premiums paid with the death benefit purchased and not with the cash value produced. The income tax advantages and the leverage of the inevitable gain make it very hard to find a compelling alternative to life insurance for the payment of estate taxes.

If the life insurance is to be used to pay estate taxes, then ownership of the insurance is very important. Either the heirs must own and pay for the insurance or it must be in an irrevocable trust. If the ownership is not set up correctly, then the proceeds from the insurance will also be taxed in the estate. Unfortunately, there are some limitations to the insurance held in a trust. Generally, annual premiums for the life insurance cannot be greater than $5,000 per beneficiary (the Crummey limitations) without beginning to use up the unified credit. Also, the insurance reverts back to the estate if the grantor insured dies within 3 years of establishing the trust or does not remove any incidents of ownership.

Many clients are willing to use up some of the credit to buy larger amounts of life insurance. The leverage of the inevitable gain may make it wiser for clients to use their credit during their lifetime through the premiums rather than through other excess lifetime gifts.

Almost always, some form of cash value policy is the most appropriate form of insurance for estate planning purposes. The fact that the problem is typically permanent lends itself to the cash value policy. Most of the clients with whom we work do not plan to die broke. If their objective is otherwise, then estate tax planning is not meaningful because they don't intend to leave a legacy anyway. For those clients who do care about their heirs, though, they usually see their estate growing for several years thereby creating a mounting estate tax concern.

If you accept the premise that the client is looking for death benefit rather than cash value, then the cost of the insurance is a critical component of the decision. All things being equal, the lowest cost permanent solution would be the best alternative. This is where the niche survivorship life (second-to-die) policy comes into play.

While there are all kinds of derivatives from this policy, the essence of the program is the recognition that one spouse can pass unlimited assets upon their death without estate tax implications to the surviving spouse. The first-to-die would typically utilize his or her full unified credit and potentially any generation-skipping options. The surviving spouse can pass whatever is left of the unified credit estate tax free, but the heirs will be responsible for taxes on the second spouse's estate above this credit. A second-to-die policy pays off on the second death, thereby creating the liquidity with which to pay the estate taxes.

The second-to-die policy is attractive because its costs are relatively low. This is because you are not insuring one life, but essentially you are insuring the life of someone other than the first to die.[1] This makes the premium costs less than the cost of separate policies. If you knew with some degree of certainty which spouse would live longer, you could buy an insurance policy only on that spouse; absent that certainty, the second-to-die policy can be quite cost-effective. If a second-to-die policy is set up appropriately in an irrevocable life insurance trust, the estate will have tremendous liquidity on the second party's death and the proceeds of the insurance are estate and income tax free.

The philosophy around owning life insurance is rather simple. It is a determination of what risks you wish to accept personally and what risks you wish to pass on. The solutions around the philosophy can be complex, and as planners we tend to complicate things even more. In determining points for the Wealth Management Index, the philosophies and strategies need to be thoroughly discussed and executed. Once this is done, your client can maximize the points in this area.

Have You Protected Yourself Against Catastrophic Loss Due to Long-Term Care, Property Losses, or Liability Issues?

The essence of financial planning is the acceptance or rejection of risk to help meet goals and objectives. We all know that every decision that we make involves some acceptance or rejection of risk. The decision to reject risk of principal by keeping money in liquid savings is by default an acceptance of the risk of loss of buying power. The key to success in financial planning is accepting only the minimum risks necessary to achieve the stated goals and objectives.

---

[1] Kenneth Black, Jr. and Harold Skipper, Jr., *Life Insurance*, 11th ed. (Englewood Cliffs, NJ: Prentice Hall, 1987), p. 77.

We need to get our clients to understand this immutable truth. One of the most meaningful pieces I have read is Sinclair Lewis' depiction of the total conformist; real estate mogul George F. Babbitt says these impassioned words to his soon-to-be son-in-law at the end of Lewis' book: "I've never done a single thing I've wanted in my whole life! I don't know's I've accomplished anything except just get along."[2] To me, that passage represents not only the quintessential risk-averse client but also most financial planning clients in general.

The most obvious area in which clients are unwilling to accept risk is in financial catastrophic planning. For Wealth Management Index purposes, because of its importance, this area represents a high nominal score, even though it can be handled quite easily and cost-effectively.

Once again, you must start off with a question: "Are you concerned with how catastrophes such as property losses, long-term care issues, or liability lawsuits could impact your financial situation?" If the client answers no, then you are done with this section, and, for your own personal liability reasons, you should probably be done with the client. It is almost impossible to justify being hired by a client for total planning and allow him or her to disregard one of the major things that could destroy all of the other work you have done. If the client answers yes, then you get to work your way down the financial catastrophe flowchart, beginning with natural disasters and ending with inadvertently spending all assets for nursing home coverage or excess medical costs.

This whole section is often only elliptically referred to in planning or even ignored, primarily because most financial planners don't feel that they have a comfortable background here or they find the subject boring. If you are unsure of yourself in this

---

[2] Sinclair Lewis, *Babbitt* (New York, Harcourt Brace Jovanovich, 1922), p. 325.

area, it is important to find someone who can help you. At Accredited Investors, Inc., we do this through strategic alliances with property/casualty experts, attorneys specializing in long-term care, and general estate planning lawyers.

Property/Casualty Insurance Property/casualty (P&C) insurance can protect clients against many of the financial catastrophes for which they cannot fully self-insure. Self-insurance is determining how much of the potential costs of claims clients wish to pay from their own assets. They may choose to fully self-insure and pay all costs or to partially self-insure by setting deductibles.

P&C decisions are often cash flow decisions. The client's ability to improve cash flow by choosing higher deductibles is one that should be weighed annually. A regular annual review of this area of the client's situation can save the client thousands of dollars over his or her lifetime.

P&C insurance does not cover all risks. Some coverage is specified perils coverage in which only certain risks are protected; other coverage is all risks coverage in which certain risks are excluded. Typically, the all risks coverage is more comprehensive. In evaluating the maximum risk that your client wishes to accept, the details of the coverage and exclusions are obviously important. It should also be noted that you cannot insure against everything that might happen. The whole P&C area is one in which pragmatism must take priority over paranoia.

Most homeowner insurance policies are written with replacement cost provisions. This basically means that after a loss, the insurance company, if the policy is set at an appropriate amount, will then pay the cost of replacing the covered property. This recognizes that even though personal property typically has dropped in value because of use, the client would still receive money to replace these goods should they be lost or stolen.

Part of a comprehensive review in this area of wealth management should include an indexing of property and a certainty that those items not covered in the base policy are provided for elsewhere. It also should include an assessment as to whether the underlying amount of property insurance is high enough to insure replacement cost. The planner should keep a copy of the client index to aid in annual reviews as well as have the client personally keep the index off-site in a safe deposit box.

Auto insurance is also an area that needs careful evaluation regularly. While responsibilities for bearing the costs of an accident vary from state to state, the two primary concerns in this area are having adequate uninsured/underinsured motorist coverage and having enough liability coverage.

In many cases, auto insurance costs should be controlled by higher deductibles which either provide an ease on cash flow or allow for greater coverage at a similar cost. Fixing a car is inconvenient; being hit by someone without insurance and being stuck paying the hospital bills could be a quasi- (or even full-blown) catastrophe. Even though other insurance the client owns (like health insurance) may cover some of these costs, if your state allows it, it is good practice to have clients' uninsured/underinsured motorist coverage match the limits established for hitting someone themselves.

Excess liability coverage is something that almost all our clients should own. The cost of this coverage is reasonable and the amount of security it provides is immense. The client also needs to be certain that his or her personal liability coverage is appropriately integrated with any professional and business liability coverage the client should own.

There are some risks that insurance may not fully be able to cover. Some clients are in high-risk-of-lawsuit occupations. According to a 1991 tape from PlainTalk, an excellent monthly compendium of financial planning issues, "38 percent of all physicians can expect to be targets of a malpractice lawsuit at some time in their careers. If the physician is a surgeon, the percentage escalates to 50 percent."[3] Obviously malpractice insurance is used to cover the cost of many of the resultant claims, but the client also needs to assess areas such as ownership of assets, corporate form, domicile, and asset transference (including trusts).

Planning for catastrophe involves an honest assessment of and decisions regarding which methods should be utilized to protect oneself from these potential risks. Just as you don't take a sledge hammer to pound in a nail, you don't immediately set up an offshore trust for a client in a high-risk occupation. The liability risks must be approached in the context of reality; the client must ultimately decide which risks are reasonable to accept.

For the client who is seriously concerned about liability risks, there are some strategies that can be incorporated into the financial plan. Typically, these ideas must be in place prior to a lawsuit being filed. Also, various states have different laws that might impede the effectiveness of a strategy.

Gifts, irrevocable trusts, family limited partnerships, and even revocable trusts for the spouse who is not likely to be sued, all provide certain advantages in making a client "judgment proof." None of these concepts is perfect. Many are merely a nuisance for creditors, thereby making it less likely for them to stake a claim. The more complex strategies should only be set up in concert with a lawyer who is experienced in these areas.

Surprisingly, some very simple tools, such as titling of assets, can provide some level of protection against creditors' claims. "Asset protection planning is the process of presenting

---

[3] PlainTalk, "Planning to Protect Personal Assets from Creditors," Program 56 (Fall City, WA: Planning Focus, Inc., 1991).

for public consumption an estate that is both modest (a relative term) and protected to a substantial extent from the claims of judgment creditors. If you are not seen as a 'deep pocket,' there is a chance you may not be sued at all."[4]

The decision around liability protection can be moralized. It is your job to bring up the concepts, whether you agree with them or not. As Atticus Finch said in Harper Lee's *To Kill a Mockingbird*, "The one thing that doesn't abide by majority rule is a person's conscience."[5] If you don't agree with what the client is doing, then you should not work with him or her. On the other hand, many conscientious clients have been damaged by improper attention to this area.

Health Care Coverage   Another area that needs to be reviewed thoroughly in the context of catastrophe planning involves medical costs. Obviously, it is the rare client that would be interested in totally self-insuring medical costs. Unfortunately, it is also possible that a client may not realize that he or she is accepting some degree of self-insurance above the deductible and co-insurance provisions with medical insurance.

It is important to pay attention to pre-existing condition clauses, basic benefit provisions (to determine which things may not be covered), as well as maximum coverage limits in determining how comprehensive the health coverage is. After fully understanding these items, you can then assess with your client how comfortable you are with the risk that he or she is assuming. For the older client, understand the Medicare benefits and integrate any supplemental coverage that may be needed.

In most cases, health care risks can be off-loaded cost-effectively to an insurance carrier. To do this, though, you need to fully understand this area.

---

[4] Ibid.

[5] Harper Lee, *To Kill a Mockingbird* (Philadelphia: Lippincott, 1960), p. 105.

Long-Term Care Coverage   Alan Parisse is a truly entertaining and informative business speaker. One of the things I heard him describe that resonated with me was his reference to how long people are living today. His said that 35 years ago when someone passed away at around age 65, people would say, "He had a good life." If that were to happen today, people would say, "He died so young."

He goes on to point out that some (not all) serious scientists (scientists, not reporters for the *National Enquirer*) suspect (not pronounce) that children born today could on average live to be 130 years old. He goes on to relate the social and psychological implications of this: euthanasia would have to be put back on the table, Social Security and Medicare would need to be completely re-evaluated, land use issues would need to be re-examined, and marriage—picture marrying at age 25 and spending the next 105 years with your spouse!

While some of those thoughts may seem far-fetched, it is true that today people are living longer than they were 35 years ago. This creates tremendous planning implications around clients outliving their assets or the potential for their assets to be completely depleted paying for nursing home costs.

If the client is concerned about this possibility, then part of the Wealth Management Index planning needs to revolve once again around asset transference issues and long-term care planning. This is an emotionally charged issue. Clients have tremendous feelings about whether family should or would take care of them should they need assisted living. Clients run the gamut regarding the ethical considerations of employing asset-shifting techniques to get the government to fund long-term care. The rules regarding these areas are dynamic and complex.

Ineffective planning in this area may not render the entire Wealth Management Index obsolete, but it can destroy much of the good that the process has brought. The costs of long-term care could deplete all of a client's assets. The decisions in this area may need to be more inclusive of other family members than any other area in the index. This is certainly true if asset shifting is desirable.

Lifelong self-sufficient clients may not be emotionally prepared to transfer assets to their children. The children may be unaware of the size of their parents' estate. The children might not be psychologically able to handle responsibilities like powers of attorney or even investment ownership. It is very often important to bring in outside professionals such as attorneys specializing exclusively in this area. Money or family therapists can also be a huge help here.

There are some basic issues to pay attention to when developing an asset-shifting strategy to qualify for Medicaid. The client needs to spend down his or her countable assets to zero to qualify for Medicaid. It is important to note, though, that some assets are not countable toward public assistance. A primary residence is not included (some states allow for more than one residence) even though it may be worth hundreds of thousands of dollars. A state can place a lien against the house to recover the cost of the nursing home care after the Medicaid recipient's death, assuming there is no surviving spouse.[6]

There is a 30-month period in which assets transferred out of the estate disqualify the client from Medicaid. Proper advance planning can enable the client to set up Medicaid trusts or other concepts to shield assets.

You can suggest long-term care insurance in addition to some form of asset shifting. This nascent area of the insurance industry is changing dramatically and will continue to do so. There haven't been enough carriers providing this long enough to establish what I feel to be credible actuarial cost assumptions. This field could end up to be like the disability insurance

---

[6] Harley Gordon, *How to Protect Your Life Savings* (Boston, MA: Financial Planning Institute, Inc., 1990), p.148.

field where the advent of noncancelable, guaranteed renewable, own-occupation policies were tremendous for sales until the claims started materializing and forced many providers out of the business. Long-term care policies are slightly different because most companies are not extended for as many potential claims as the disability carriers had been, but caution is prudent here.

In evaluating policies, you do want guaranteed renewable provisions, inflation adjustments, and potential payment for assisted daily living (ADL) problems rather than just long-term confinement. The client pays for these options, though. These policies have tremendous flexibility with regard to self-insuring because the client determines how long he or she wants the benefits to last and when they would begin. This is especially useful for planning around the time limitation on asset shifting.

Since whether the client has been institutionalized before he or she begins to shift assets is not relevant, a long-term care policy allows the client to maintain control of countable assets until they can be transferred. Any transfer of assets will disqualify the client from receiving Medicaid benefits for 30 months, but the long-term care policy can help buy the client time for planning.

There are other information resources for this long-term care planning. The U.S. Department of Health and Human Services can provide you with information on Medigap coverage. Many states can also offer information on long-term care, although states are not enamored with asset shifting because they bear the costs of those without the resources to pay for care themselves.

Catastrophe planning is clearly an extremely important component of the Wealth Management Index. Again, you and the client need to make decisions around the risks that he or she is willing to assume. It is not the decisions around the risk that the client is willing to assume that will garner the points for the index but rather the effective implementation of solutions for those decisions.

Are Your Business Interests Adequately Covered?

Many of our clients own businesses and don't even realize it. For those clients whose principal income source is their service or manufacturing company, being a business owner is almost self-defining. But what about the day care facility operator who personally owns the real estate that she leases back to her company or the doctor who helps finance a friend's start-up business? These clients own businesses which must be reviewed in order to fully understand their opportunities and exposure in accumulating wealth.

In your initial fact-gathering meeting with the client, obvious business interests will be discussed. In working with the client in this area, though, more subtle interests can be uncovered from tax returns. Form K-1 will tell you what real estate is owned and in what other partnerships or corporations the client may be involved. This information will also reveal the extent of material participation in any companies. Even general dividend and capital gain schedules might identify loans made that could have some business purpose and, hence, consequences.

As this unravels, you need to establish whether these business interests are in the appropriate form. Businesses comprise one of three forms or a derivative of these: a sole proprietorship, a partnership (general, limited, or limited liability), or a corporation (C, S, personal service, or limited liability).

There are many reasons why a particular type of business form is more or less appropriate. The pure C-corporation is the most different from the others in that this is the only structure that is not a pass-through entity. Again, a PlainTalk tape program gives an excellent overview of business structure and discusses twelve factors in determining this:

1. Future potential sale.
2. Different ownership interests.
3. Limited liability.
4. Earnings bail out (getting money out).
5. Conversion ability.
6. Tax brackets on net earned income.
7. Loss utilizations.
8. Fringe benefits.
9. Qualified retirement plans.
10. Tax deferral.
11. Passive activity rules.
12. Alternative minimum tax.[7]

Limited liability corporations (LLCs) have begun to take the place of S-corporations for many small business owners because, among other things, they allow more flexibility in ownership. While this concept is intriguing, for a client who operates in more than one state, the LLC will not provide adequate protection from liability.

One of the exciting things about working with business owners is that they recognize risk. German poet Frederich Von Schiller said in *Fiesco,* "To save all we must risk all."[8] Business owners have grasped the concept of their own destiny and risk all to make their mark. This leaves them vulnerable to not adequately assessing risks other than business risks. For this part

---

[7] PlainTalk, "Choosing the Best Business Form," Program 69 (Fall City, WA: Planning Focus, Inc., 1992).

[8] Frederich Von Schiller, *Fiesco,* in *The Columbia Dictionary of Quotations,* ed. Robert Andrews (New York: Columbia University Press, 1993), p. 792.

of the Wealth Management Index, anyone with a business inter-est must make determinations about a variety of things.

After you have decided upon an appropriate business struc-ture, you then need to have the client establish a business valu-ation. Even if the business is a sole proprietorship, it makes sense to regularly establish a value for the business. If there is a non-active spouse in the business, an appropriate valuation can give him or her some reasonable starting point if the client dies. A regular valuation is essential in effective estate planning and is very useful in long-range planning for corporate form and deter-mining exit strategies.

There is a wide variety of ways to value a business and I firmly believe that this should be done by someone with the expertise to consider all the nuances of business ownership. The ramifications of a shoddily done valuation could be far more costly than the costs of a competent appraiser. For example, we work with someone who became our client after he bought a manufacturing company. The poor due diligence on his appraisal of the company resulted in his substantially overpaying for equip-ment that was close to obsolete.

Michael Porter's book *Competitive Strategy*[9] is a valuable resource for looking at businesses (especially manufacturing companies) and understanding their strategic direction and the potential threats they face. While this book won't help you give an appraisal on the client's business, it will help you be conver-sant regarding potentials and pitfalls.

If the business has more than one owner (or if there is some-one who will logically buy the business should the owner pass away), the next step is to have a buy/sell document drawn. This is an area that is crucial for the overall financial (and emotional) well-being of the client.

---

[9] Michael Porter, *Competitive Strategy* (New York: Free Press, 1980).

Buy/sells have two major purposes: to maintain control of the business and to provide liquidity for owners who are leaving. Well-crafted buy/sells also have a third, often inarticulated, purpose: they force the owners of the business to think toward the future and encourage them to determine how they will work together in bad times. The buy/sell for my business took 2 years for Wil and me to complete because it constantly brought up new issues regarding our partnership. While it was at times painful, it was eminently rewarding and prudent.

Buy/sells help maintain control of the business because they establish parameters around issues such as who can own the business, what the transition strategy is for the owners, and how a forced liquidation of the business can be avoided. Buy/sells are crucial in S-corporations to prevent an unsuitable owner (a trust, a foreign spouse) from jeopardizing the S-corp status.

There are many other things that need careful analysis with regard to buy/sells, but one of the more interesting ideas is that of a showdown clause whereby an owner who wants to leave states a price for the company and the remaining owners either have to pay it or sell their interests to the other owner at that price. Some other important and complicated areas that need to be explored are corporate responsibilities during incapacity or when shareholders or partners become incompetent.

The buy/sell cannot be shelved once it is written. The reason it has a role in the Wealth Management Index is because of the need to not only write it but also to regularly review it. Businesses change every year and some of the most well-designed buy/sells may be outdated rather quickly. While most agreements can be written in a manner that allows the business to change, a regular review is still recommended.

Last, an unfunded buy/sell is virtually meaningless. Without a plan in place to fund an owner's departure or to provide income to a deceased owner's heirs, the buy/sell is an exercise in futility.

There are many ways to provide funding for a buy/sell. While life insurance is often the most appropriate (and usually the most cost-effective) method for the other owners to directly purchase the deceased owner's interests from the estate (stock purchase plan) or for the corporation to purchase the stock directly (stock redemption), ideas such as installment sales or ESOPs may also be explored.

Just as the second-to-die life insurance policy is an attractive niche for estate planning, a first-to-die life insurance policy may be useful for business planning. This is especially true in stock redemption buy/sells. The insurance pays upon the death of the first shareholder, thereby infusing the company with cash to buy the stock from the shareholder's estate.

While first-to-die is less expensive than separate policies, its mortality structure is not nearly as attractive as second-to-die because you are actually increasing the risk to the insurance company by paying on the first life. Also, these policies are not very good if the partnership or company breaks up. While there are riders that you can add to the policy to allow for new insureds should a shareholder leave or should one buy into the company, these policies may still not be flexible enough for solving business problems.

Often it makes sense to own key person insurance (potentially through a split dollar program) coupled with the buy/sell insurance. This allows for the value of the company to be reduced to help accurately reflect the cost of the lost owner, yet it does not force the surviving spouse to live off a ridiculously low stock payment. While this can provide some estate tax savings to the surviving heirs, it may not help the existing shareholders with a significantly higher stepped-up basis in the stock they just purchased. Clearly the scope of these decisions cannot be adequately covered in this book.

Installment sales involve the buying of the business over time. They are often funded on a pay-as-you-go basis and can therefore cause a financial strain on the company. Installment sales are attractive to sellers because it can allow them to defer some of their gains and to receive a competitive interest rate on the money owed to them.

ESOPs also may provide some liquidity for the selling shareholder although they are expensive to maintain.

Summary

The value of the asset protection component of the Wealth Management Index is that it clearly gives the client a baseline for security that no other area can offer. Absent a strong asset protection plan, clients who have done well in the other areas of the index could still find themselves destitute. The costs to be properly set up in this area are nominal compared to the costs of not adequately performing here.

CASE STUDY

FACTS

A couple, Dr. Susan Charles, a radiologist, and her husband, Jeffrey Charles, a writer, are both in their late 40s. They have no children, nor do they plan to have any.

Dr. Charles makes $350,000 a year and Mr. Charles makes $10,000 annually. Dr. Charles does not like what she does and would like to "retire" and go into teaching in 5 years.

They have considerable assets, both personally and in Dr. Charles' retirement plan. Dr. Charles is a shareholder in her professional corporation and a general partner in a building in which they practice. Mr. Charles is a self-employed freelance writer.

While the Charleses came to us primarily for asset management, the development of the Wealth Management Index for the asset protection area reveals some key issues which will be discussed and scored at the end of the year.

The areas of asset protection for the Wealth Management Index follow:

1. Are your business interests adequately covered?
   - Are all of the Charleses' businesses in appropriate form?
   - Have the businesses been valued properly?
   - Have buy/sell agreements been established and reviewed?
   - Has funding for these agreements been established?
2. Do you have an appropriate amount of life insurance consistent with an articulated philosophy around this insurance?
   - What is the necessary level of support for each of the Charleses' should one predecease the other?
   - What is the current structure of the assets the Charleses currently have and what is the anticipated growth of these?
   - How do the Charleses feel about paying estate taxes?
3. Have you protected yourself against catastrophic loss due to long-term care, property losses, or liability issues?
   - What are the parameters and selection of property/casualty insurance for this wealthy couple?
   - Is it important to review long-term care issues?
   - What types of asset transference may be appropriate?

SCORING FOR THE WEALTH MANAGEMENT INDEX

Throughout the year, these various areas were discussed and decisions were made that are comfortable for the clients. This is how the scoring went.

Business Form

Dr. Charles had little control over the business form of her practice. It was established as a professional corporation and the other physicians wished to keep it like this. It was determined, though, that equipment that was not leased through the practice should potentially be bought through another entity formed by the doctors.

We also reviewed the potential problems of the general partnership on the real estate. While the financing of the property is nonrecourse, there is still exposure on any other debts incurred by any of the general partners in the program, as well as some potential personal liability issues on accidents or claims that occur at the partnership level.

It was decided to convert the general partnership to a limited liability partnership. In essence, for a small amount of money, a corporate "shield" can be bought. The limited partnership agreements were checked to see if there were any troublesome agreements that would preclude this conversion. The bank was also willing to reassign the debt to the new entity (the creation of the entity does not release any of the partners from debt obligations already incurred). Minnesota is a state in which the laws for LLPs are favorable; if they weren't, an LLC might have needed to have been explored.

Mr. Charles operates as a sole proprietor. He has no inventory and operates as a cash-basis taxpayer. He deposits all his earnings into a segregated account and pays for all business expenses through this account.

This entity has no insulation from liability. If he wants to expand his writing into a product (such as a self-published book), he may wish to change his form because of inventory issues. Since he is the only person in the business, an LLP cannot be done. He did not feel comfortable becoming an S-corporation, and since he conducts business in several states, an LLC was somewhat impractical.

Appropriate business form represents 2.8 points of the index. (There are 25 total points for asset protection with business interests representing 34 percent of this. Business form accounts for 33 percent of this 34 percent: $100 \times \{(.25 \times .34) \times .33\}$.)

Since all areas were thoroughly discussed and implemented, the Charleses received the full 2.8 points.

Buy/Sell and Valuation

We reviewed the buy/sells on the professional corporation. There are both death and disability buyout provisions that seem adequate. There are also provisions for leaving the practice early. Funding is through a combination of cash flow and insurance.

There was not a recent valuation done for the real estate, and the buy/sell also needed to be revamped to reflect the entity change. There were also no guarantees that if Dr. Charles were to leave the practice and wished to sell her interest in the building that the bank would release her of her debt obligations. A new valuation for the building was done which reflected a substantial increase in the value of the property. A provision was placed in the buy/sell to update the appraisal every 2 years.

With Dr. Charles' desire to leave early, the financial strength of the other people in the partnership becomes important. The bank would be more inclined to release Dr. Charles if the other investors' balance sheets were sufficient to support the buyout of her position (potentially through new financing). Provisions were put in place to share this sensitive, yet germane, information with each other.

Establishing and funding the buy(keep)/sells represents 4.25 points $(100 \times \{(.25 \times .34) \times .5\})$. All 4.25 points were earned.

Business valuation is worth 1.4 points $(100 \times \{(.25 \times .34) \times .17\})$. All points were earned here.

Support after Death

This area involved lengthy discussions throughout the year. The Charleses have no children, have all four of their parents living, and have no other siblings to which they wish to leave a big estate. They are both active in their alma maters.

We based our expectations for the Wealth Management Index on what they told us during our meetings. They indicated that they wanted the surviving spouse to maintain the same lifestyle should one of them die. We also know that their assets need to grow rapidly enough in the next few years to support a much reduced earned income level when Dr. Charles goes into teaching.

The death capital needs analysis (DCNA) run for the Charleses showed no insurance needed on Mr. Charles but a significant amount necessary on Dr. Charles. This was after factoring in the buy/sell insurance available. It was also determined, though, that Dr. Charles would like to quit working immediately upon the death of Mr. Charles. Essentially, this created a need for life insurance on Mr. Charles similar to the level needed on Dr. Charles.

Since the Charleses' assets are growing rapidly and they save a substantial amount of Dr. Charles' income already, it won't be long before their assets will be sufficient to support Mr. Charles should Dr. Charles pass away. This means that their lifestyle protection needs for insurance will drop significantly over time.

Neither of the couple cares at all about estate taxes. They intend to make their alma maters the benefactor of most of their money.

Once it was time to purchase the term insurance deemed necessary from the DCNA and the other discussions, Dr. Charles hesitated on her previous statement about retiring should something happen to Mr. Charles. For scoring for the Wealth Management Index, we had to reduce their points here, because it was impossible to distinguish whether this hesitancy was due to the cost of the insurance or a change in her feelings about work. While we can change the goal on next year's Wealth Management Index, for this year points must be sacrificed.

Providing support and accurately reflecting the use of their assets represented a possible 7.43 points ($100 \times \{(.25 \times .33) \times .9\}$). Since the Charleses did fully fund the insurance on Dr. Charles but not on Mr. Charles, they lost half of the funding points. Their total here then was 5.56 points.

They fully realized the estate tax points because they are unconcerned with the estate tax issue. They therefore received .825 points here ($100 \times \{(.25 \times .33) \times .1\}$).

Property/Casualty

The P&C review resulted in significant changes. Their personal umbrella liability policy was increased from $1 million to $3 million. We also filed an inventory of their personal belongings. The Charleses' earned all 4.125 points ($100 \times \{(.25 \times .33) \times .5\}$).

Long-Term Care

The Charleses did not feel that planning was needed for the long-term care at this time. Since the subject was fully discussed, they earned 2.06 points ($100 \times \{(.25 \times .33) \times .25\}$).

Asset Transference

The most significant change here was the ownership of more assets in Mr. Charles' name as a way to somewhat (albeit not very effectively) protect their assets should a claim be made on the real estate or the medical practice. They understood that asset protection procedures need to be done prior to a lawsuit being filed. They did not feel that doing anything more exotic was necessary at that time. They scored 2.06 points ($100 \times \{(.25 \times .33) \times .25\}$).

SUMMARY

The Charleses earned 23.13 points out of a possible 25. Since planning is fluid, some of the areas that needed no attention this year may become more important in the ensuing years. Therefore, all of these items need to be addressed regularly.

Also, recognize that objectives may change throughout the year. We need to score based on objectives established early on. Those that change will be reflected in a later year's plan. This is so current scoring cannot be manipulated by changes.

5

DISABILITY AND INCOME PROTECTION (PROTECTION)

While we label this component of the Wealth Management Index "Protection", this word is extended to its highest and greatest use. It represents more than protecting a loss of income from disability. It also includes protecting the client's cash flow through disciplined and conscientious budgeting, monitoring "under-earning," and actively pursuing means to protect the client's earned income from unacceptable tax consequences.

Completely understanding sources of revenues and actively planning to spend according to the client's values protects him or her from the unwanted consequences of not investing according to plan and therefore ultimately not providing for an adequate lifestyle for today or tomorrow.

This section in financial planning can be compared with the annual checkup in medicine: once you have completed it and have been prescribed your diet and exercise regime, it often is a matter of time before you grab for the candy instead of the couscous or perform thumb presses on the remote rather than bench presses in the gym. You see, this is the section of the financial plan that includes the budget. It is dedicated to understanding what amount of money comes into your client's accounts throughout the year and where that money goes. It is the section that also establishes some minimum level of receipts should our clients become disabled.

We also evaluate taxes here—an area that I have yet to have a client indicate a wish not to control when we first meet. This is one particular section where expectation management is crucial due to the limitations on the exotic planning that was done prior to the tax reform in 1986.

Potential inheritances and retirement income numbers are discussed here. This is again where some of those nefarious long-range projections enter into the plan.

Most important, this is the hub around which planning revolves. While it often seems relatively easy and is treated somewhat perfunctorily, this part of the plan will establish our opportunities for success in all other areas of the plan.

Percent of Index (20%) for Disability and Income Protection (Protection)

	Percent of Disability and Income Protection Scale	Total Index Weight
Do you have too much or too little disability protection given your assets and income and will it pay you should you be unable to work?	40%	8%
Did you receive in income from all sources (earnings, gifts, social security, pensions) what you expected to this year?	20	4
Did you spend according to plan?	20	4
Did you use all reasonable means to reduce your taxes?	20	4

Values Planning (Cash Flow)

Over the years we have called budgets many things to try to mask their true identity. We do this because for most clients, the word *budget* conjures up all sorts of negative images and emotions. Even so, cash flows make budgets seem corporate and impersonal, inflow and outflow analyses make them completely clinical, and the term *spending policy* seems somewhat obtuse.

Budgets really are values assessments for the client. They detail what the client feels is most important by the spending choices he or she (somewhat) consciously makes. The pain of the budget is that all too often these spending choices seem to conflict with other expressed goals or values. It is this juxtaposition of words versus deeds that causes the discomfort which can make us tacitly approve this area by not challenging our clients.

Wealth management is inexorably tied into the values planning process. Every spending decision made (or avoided) today leads to a very different outcome in the future because of the elements of time and compound interest. On the other hand, investing-only decisions today could lead to a suppressed lifestyle that creates disutility between enjoying the moment and the fear of not being able to enjoy it tomorrow. This is the dead bird in the hand approach—living an austere existence so that later spending patterns can completely change. Frugality will lead to frivolity. For most clients, though, this spending epiphany is not ever realized.

As you begin to work through the index with your client, the questioning process must deal with all the mixed feelings that money brings. This discovering process will better help you create benchmarks with your clients consistent with their living (not just expressed) values.

Did You Receive in Income (Earnings, Gifts, Social Security, Pension) What You Expected to This Year?

A surprising number of clients have not evaluated closely all areas of income potential, the most basic first step to wealth management. Especially for business owners, income can come from many different sources and can also be difficult to predict. Income planning must be both retrospective, to try to garner information on all avenues of money coming in, and prospective, to give an honest evaluation of which new sources of funds will be available or which old sources may be changing.

For the Wealth Management Index, the client must first establish the income or cash inflow number off which they expect to be working. This number is the benchmark against which income success is evaluated.

While earnings are the most obvious and usually the primary source of income, other areas should also be identified. Clients who are approaching retirement or who have accumulated large sums in their retirement plans and could be facing excise tax consequences need to make conscious decisions about whether those plans should be invaded. While most of the time it will make sense to continue to defer, the review should be performed regularly. After a couple of years of exceptional investment performance, the previously innocuous excise tax issue may be more imposing.

Clients who have earned pensions and have flexibility with when they can take them should be evaluating those decisions annually. We have found with some clients that for many years we had planned on taking either a single or joint life annuity option on their pension plan, yet because interest rates dropped so significantly over the last few years, it made far more sense to roll over the lump sum and either spend down other assets or take substantially equal payments out of the rolled-over IRA.

Deploying the substantially equal payments strategy does not have to be an all or nothing choice. If a client has more than one IRA established, you may use that planning tool on any or all of them. This splitting of IRAs enables the client to manage cash flow while still having assets grow to retirement.

Clients may also have qualified for retirement benefits in other countries in which they worked. One client, a football coach for many years in Canada, was eligible for reduced benefits from the Canadian equivalent of the US Social Security system.

Other areas of income should also be explored. Inheritance and gifts are becoming a large part of planning for middle-aged clients. While many clients don't wish to consider the potential for gifts or inheritance in their planning, it nonetheless does impact long-term planning because of estate or divorce issues as well as current planning from an income and tax standpoint. When performing family planning for an elderly parent with a middle-aged child, coordinated gift planning can be an almost magical tool.

Investments cannot be discounted when doing income evaluations. Even if the client does not intend to draw from these investments, he or she will create sources of capital that, depending on where the client is in his or her life cycle, may be advantageous to use. More important, a client may correctly choose to spend principal rather than to sell appreciated investments or to spend principal outside retirement plans rather than to invade those plans.

A full understanding of all potential sources of cash inflow is what is required to maximize potential points in this category. This complete awareness of the income that the client will be receiving will launch the budget work and provide the grounding for the spending decisions.

Did You Spend According to Plan?

The cash flow evaluation is important to the Wealth Management Index concept because we need to understand our clients' values to initially set the relevant benchmarks or goals. We also need to have a feel for what a client spends so that we can accurately determine the amount of disability, life, and savings needs he or she has to insure the realization of those goals. Not spending the front time on this values area is guaranteed to result in a plan that will not be on point.

The conflict that many clients have between what they verbalize and what they do is a struggle that all financial planners face in the quest to put together responsive and individualized plans. The struggle manifests itself in clients who declare their comfort with volatility risk, only to be found hyperventilating during market drops. Unfortunately, we often can't uncover this risk misunderstanding until it may be too late. The cash flow inconsistencies can be detected immediately. This may help provide clues of conflict in other areas.

One of the nicest things about uncovering cash flow inconsistencies is that this may help you identify your own clients' understanding about their financial conditions. Those who talk about wanting to live a better lifestyle today yet valiantly latch onto each dollar, in much the same way as my rotweiller clings to his bones, are probably more closely aligned with a fear-based profile than a greedy one. They hold onto the money because they fear it might go away, not because they are so avaricious that parting with it causes consternation. Those who spend well beyond what they claim they value are probably closer to a greedy or relationship client than a curious or fear-based one.

I recently had an anesthesiologist prospect in my office who in the span of about an hour and a half made a multitude of conflicting statements to me. He started the conversation by talking about how his business is changing and that he anticipates a 30 percent drop in income in his practice within 5 years.

He went on to say that he doesn't want his lifestyle to change in spite of this income drop. He just recently built a house that went over budget by about $200,000 so he wanted to sell his investments to pay down the mortgage (in anticipation of this cash shortage). Retirement planning was of major importance and private school for his three children was a must.

After listening and trying not to judge, I repeated back to him what I had heard his goals to be and he began to laugh. I explained that there were many things that we could do together if we could get good clarity on his situation, including cash flow. He didn't believe in budgets because they are too confining. Since he was making over $300,000 dollars a year, he didn't feel that a cash flow analysis would be helpful. He just wanted me to advise him on what to do.

I almost felt like the "olden days" in theater when the deus ex machina descended from the ceiling to solve a convoluted plot. I ended up letting him know that I was sensitive to his plight, but that I didn't believe that I could ultimately help him unless we began at the beginning, something he refused to do. There are days when I regret that I don't manage his significant retirement plan, but those regrets are tempered by thinking about the pressure I would have been placed under to direct but not evaluate. I think that I was able to avoid the inevitable pain of dealing with a greedy client.

Even with the less spendthrifty and more sophisticated clients, cash flow should be reviewed. The point is not to necessarily fine tune the outflow, but it is to understand the values around that outflow and attempt to eliminate the discord between actions and values. Oscar Wilde described cynics as "People who know the price of everything and the value of nothing."[1] We must understand the client's values so as to not be cynics.

---

[1] Oscar Wilde, *The Picture of Dorian Gray* (New York: Penguin Classics, 1985), p. 71.

Cash flow planning of the future will involve setting our clients up on a program such as Quicken, and either inputting the data ourselves (maybe through independent contractors) or by having the clients input their own information. A disk can be exchanged each quarter prior to the meeting so an understanding can be had of the cash flow choices to date. To the extent that those choices are inconsistent with stated values, a discussion must ensue to determine whether objectives need to be modified or the plan needs to be altered. Unfortunately, until the day comes when all of our clients walk in with the cash outflow artfully prepared on the computer, we will need to help them prepare these data.

The evaluative need here is to spend according to plan. There are a number of items which surface in any year that could cause a sea change in spending. Those items which are unexpected yet necessary (furnace repairs, a car being totaled, etc.) would reduce the client's Wealth Management Index score only slightly (and not at all if appropriate emergency funds were established). Those items that were not considered in the beginning of the year but were used as a reward (lavish trips, new car) would point out the lack of congruence between the client's stated values and actions and would therefore be penalized more harshly for Wealth Management Index scoring purposes.

The interplay between you and your client around what constitutes a necessary expenditure is never completely comfortable. Clients frequently rationalizing their purchases is really a cry for help—help that is sometimes awkward to deliver.

There is the story of the man who suffered such a tremendous financial setback that he could not land back on his feet. He finally turned to God.

"God," he prayed, "you've got to help me. The only way I can get back on my feet is if I win the lottery. Please make me win."

This went on for a few days. The man didn't think that God was hearing him. He was getting desperate. Almost hopeless, he again turned to God. "I beg of you, dear God. All I need is to win the lottery."

After a moment of silence a voice came back to him saying, "Give me a break. At least buy a ticket."

This values assessment in the Wealth Management Index is in essence the lottery ticket for which the beggar was crying. We cannot help our clients reach their ultimate financial goals unless we help them purchase the ticket to do so.

For Wealth Management Index purposes, the cash outflow assessment will also be important in the investment planning section, as 40 percent of that area is determining whether the client has set aside what he or she had anticipated.

Do You Have Too Much or Too Little Disability Protection Given Your Assets and Income and Will It Pay You Should You Be Unable to Work?

Once the cash flow has been produced and you have evaluated it, you can then make a determination as to whether the client has enough assets to support him- or herself should he or she be unable to work. If the answer is yes, a discussion must still take place around whether the client wishes to use these assets for this purpose. If the client is comfortable spending current assets to pay for personal incapacity, then this piece of the index is done and a score can be granted.

Most clients will either not have the assets (especially if they are young, high-income earners) or would rather explore alternatives to using current dollars. For these clients, disability insurance must be pursued. If the client can obtain disability insurance, the evaluative process of amount and type of coverage can begin.

The DCNA provides a mechanism to determine an estimate of the life insurance need that a client has. A similar type of analysis can be done for disability planning. In the initial meeting you discovered what the client's goals were and the things that he or she was willing to give up to achieve them. In subsequent meetings you developed an understanding of how congruent the client's spending is with his or her expressed objectives. The synchronicity between the long-term goals and the current spending patterns forms the basis for the disability income needs analysis.

In most circumstances, regardless of how this analysis plays out, the client will be interested in obtaining the largest amount of disability protection available. While that conservative position can be defensible, it is not always the best decision. Obviously anyone that is disabled would not be interested in turning aside benefit, but until that occurs, the reasonableness test must still apply.

Like catastrophe planning issues, it most likely makes sense to self-insure those events that would be uncomfortable but not devastating. For disability income purposes, this would usually mean that the client (depending on occupation) should extend the waiting period (the amount of time before the disability begins to pay) to at least 90 days. For example, a business owner may have set up the company in such a manner that his salary can continue for a period of time even if he is unable to work. Physician or attorney groups should have provisions in their buy/sells as well as general policies that establish how long the other physicians or partners will "carry" the disabled professional. Costs can drop considerably by choosing to self-insure over a longer waiting period.

The catastrophe that must be avoided is the cost of not insuring a long-term, debilitating disability. The average duration of a disability that lasts at least 90 days is 5 years. Protecting against that kind of loss is crucial for overall wealth management.

Since you are protecting the client from a long-term disability, the amount of disability insurance that you need must factor in savings numbers for retirement or other items. There are some limitations as to the total amount of coverage someone may purchase, but for the cases where you are evaluating owning even less than this amount, the tweaking should still allow for a set-aside.

Also, it makes no sense to purchase a long-term disability policy without also including a cost of living rider. You have not adequately protected the client if you only insure current income and let inflation ravage his or her spending power.

Many clients have the choice of purchasing a disability policy with pretax dollars, thereby rendering the benefit taxable, or after-tax dollars, where the benefit is then paid tax free. We almost always encourage our clients to pay their premiums with after-tax dollars, although it could be argued that the premium is certain while the benefit is uncertain. Once again, if the issue that is of greatest concern is long-term disability, then the years of tax-free payments will more than make up for the tax cost on the premiums paid.

Future income options are also important additions to most policies. The future purchase option will allow the client to purchase more coverage without qualifying through a physical (although he or she will most likely need to income-justify the purchase). It stands to reason that the uninsurable client has a higher risk of disability, hence the uninsurability. This option will lay that issue aside.

The most important components of a disability contract are the definition of disability and the renewability and cancelability of the policy. A noncancelable, guaranteed renewable policy means that as long as the client pays the premiums, he or she will be covered. Also, no matter how bad the risk pool of the insurance company is, premiums cannot be raised.

The definition of disability is important because of all the nuances around this. For example, some policies have an income determinant rather than or in addition to a time-lost determinant. Professionals who bill for their services after the tasks are completed might not suffer a loss of income until several months after they are disabled.

Also, some policies have an any-occupation rather than an own-occupation clause in the contract. Professionals covered under an any-occupation definition may be able to perform some job other than that for which they were trained, thereby rendering them unable to obtain benefits.

Group policies offered through companies are almost always less expensive than private programs—with good reason. Most group policies are much more restrictive, often limiting own-occupation after a 2-year period, neither providing much inflation protection nor noncancelable or guaranteed renewable features. Most professionals, in spite of the extra cost, should own individual coverage.

The disability policy needs to be reviewed to be sure the coverage is of top quality. Disability costs go up each year, so the cost of switching policies is most likely the cost associated with being older and a greater risk. In spite of these costs, if the client does not have top-quality coverage, it should either be obtained by changing the current coverage or, at worst, integrating a high-quality policy with the existing plan.

Disability coverage is changing dramatically. Many of the historically strongest companies in this area are either no longer in it or have changed their coverage so that it is no longer attractive. Because of this, you cannot delay in carefully covering this area for your client.

Uninsurability What if the client is uninsurable? While high-quality private insurance may not be an option, obviously the availability of group insurance through work or associations and the future purchase options on existing coverage should be explored. You can also see whether the client is able to add a disability waiver on his or her life insurance. This would serve to pay the policy premiums and, if it is a superfunded policy, may over time give the client access to cash.

The business owner may see whether business overhead coverage is available under slightly less stringent underwriting criteria. Products that normally are terrible buys—credit disability insurance on a car loan or mortgage, for example—may now have some appeal.

Since the nature of this ancillary coverage will not be as good as private coverage, the client needs to prepare to self-fund some needs. This speaks to being certain that maximum credit lines are established and paying close attention to the marketability of the client investment portfolio. While you can't go overboard by converting all investments to cash, the uninsurable client is definitely at higher risk of not fulfilling wealth management goals and planning must recognize this.

Did You Use All Reasonable Means to Reduce Your Taxes?

"Man . . . cannot learn to forget, but hangs on the past: however far or fast he runs, that chain runs with him."[2] Nietzsche may not have been talking about tax reform when he uttered those comments, but he might as well have been. How many clients

---

[2] Frederich Nietzsche, *The Use and Abuse of History*, in *The Columbia Dictionary of Quotations*, ed. Robert Andrews (New York: Columbia University Press, 1993), p. 671.

come traipsing into your office stating that they pay too much in taxes as their primary concern? People still cling to those past planning techniques that transformed income taxes into tax deductions. They tend to forget that the chain of events continued into tax loss carryforwards and eventually into phantom income.

Tax planning is necessary and appropriate in quality financial planning. Unfortunately, it just isn't as cute as it used to be. As we proceed along the inexorable march to the land of the flat tax, creativity will probably be diminished further. Income tax planning only has a relative value of 4 percent on the total Wealth Management Index because of its present and future limitations.

Tax planning begins with a tax assessment. This objective evaluation determines what your client would pay without any preventative steps. These tax estimates ideally should be performed in the year for which the client will be paying taxes so that some planning can take place. In fact, in October you will begin to be able to guess what kind of income your client will have, what types of gains the client's mutual funds may be distributing, how much of the Section 179 expense has been utilized, where the client is at on charitable contributions, and whether enough state tax will have been withheld.

The key reason for doing a tax estimate is to understand the marginal federal tax bracket the client is in and the relative danger of being in alternative minimum tax. For clients who have significant stock options or have income and expense control of their businesses, this information may be one of the last bastions of true tax strategizing. (Note: I do recognize that certain business planning may allow for a tremendous amount of tax panache.)

Once this information is known, it is best to start with the basics and then move to the sublime. The easiest piece of wealth management is determining whether there will be any change in marginal bracket from the current year to the next. Obviously you wish to bring taxable income into the low-bracket years and send deductible expenses into the higher-bracket years.

While this concept appears rudimentary, a surprising number of people miss this with regard to retirement planning distributions. This is especially important in the year in which a minimum distribution is required because you have the choice of straddling two tax years. Also, the retiree who has substantial plan assets yet little other income may wish to bring in income to maximize the lower bracket.

Another basic thing to pay attention to is the ability to itemize deductions. This is very important for those clients who are determining whether a mortgage payoff makes sense. Clients (especially in high income tax states) may have been itemizing primarily because of their state income tax deduction. When they retire and have converted earned income to tax-favored income, the state tax deduction may have dropped enough so that the clients are barely able to itemize. These clients need to evaluate bunching deductions and paying off debt so as to maximize their tax leverage.

While most people spend time thinking about their itemized deductions, close attention must be paid to above-the-line income and deductions (things that reduce adjusted gross income) from below-the-line deductions (things that reduce taxable income). Above-the-line income could impair the amount of below-the-line deductions for which a client is eligible. Above-the-line deductions are not subjected to phase-out restrictions. This means that most high-income clients should be maximizing their cafeteria plans, funding retirement programs, and aggressively monitoring their investment portfolios to best manage this item.

Investments should also be viewed relative to their tax efficiency. Unfortunately, the research on tax-managing mutual fund portfolios is relatively unclear. A recent essay in the *No-Load Fund Analyst* showed little movement among ranking of funds after you take into account tax impact.[3]

Intuitive judgments regarding tax efficiency of mutual funds are also not always accurate. For example, studies have shown that any portfolio turnover ratio greater than 15 percent has relatively the same tax consequence. The theory, then, of value funds being more tax efficient than growth funds is not valid.

Also, while individually managed portfolios of stocks can be more efficient than a similarly managed mutual fund portfolio, a recent Bernstein study does not show appreciable differences between the two.[4]

Asset transference is another way to reduce taxes. Transferring ownership of stocks or mutual funds to children can allow them to earn income otherwise taxed to you. Tax reform has made UTMAs slightly less attractive for children under 14, but minor's trusts still allow for greater income-shifting possibilities. Unfortunately, the end game for income shifting is typically education costs. Dollars in the children's names are treated more importantly for financial aid qualification than money kept in a parent's name. Therefore, control and end use must be weighed against the ever-decreasing tax advantages.

Stock option planning will become increasingly important. The old rule of thumb was to encourage clients to wait as long as possible to exercise their stock options to delay the tax bite as long as possible. With the tremendous difference between income tax and capital gains tax, and the added responsibility placed on high-level employees to keep a certain amount of company stock, this argument is somewhat specious.

---

[3] Ken Gregory and Craig Litman, editors, "Evaluating Stock Funds: How Important Are Taxes?" *No-Load Fund Analyst*, November 1995.
[4] *Taxes and the Private Investor* (New York: Sanford C. Bernstein & Co., Inc., 1995).

For example, we have a client who owns considerable stock options in a very thinly traded public company with over 60 percent family ownership. The patriarch of the family is almost 70 years old and there are no children interested in taking over the business. The business is a monopoly in the city in which it operates, is trading at almost 40 percent of book value (because trades occur only intermittently throughout the month), and is trading at 4 times earnings in an industry where the average multiple has been between 11 and 19. It is highly likely that the family will be disengaging their ownership of the stock over the next few years by creating a more public market.

In this case, the client is better served by exercising and holding onto his stock so as to convert what would be huge ordinary income into more favored long-term gains. Granted, there is still some price and tax uncertainty in this, but the probability of this being appropriate outweighs that uncertainty.

Timing of income and expenses is a key planning area for those with businesses. Generally, all things being equal, it is better to pay a tax tomorrow rather than today. Cash-basis taxpayers have more flexibility with regard to these timing issues than do those who are accrual based.

It is appropriate to sit down with your business-owner clients to be certain that they take full advantage of these timing issues by maximizing their Section 179 expense deductions, prepaying those items that would qualify for expensing, and determining whether any income can be received the following year without violating the principal of constructive receipt. Business owners do need to pay close attention to lowering the income to the point where they may violate any loan covenants that they may have or impair their ability to fund their retirement plans to the optimum level.

Another item to explore with corporate clients is the opportunity to participate in deferred compensation or supplemental employee retirement programs (SERP). These programs typically need an adequate amount of time for the benefits to be valuable, which opens the client up to two risks: (1) the risk that the company won't be around to pay the deferred compensation, and (2) the risk that tax laws will change and make a reasonable current strategy seem unreasonable.

Companies like deferred compensation plans because they tie the employee to the company. These plans are also not subjected to discrimination testing so the benefits can be delivered to only the people the company chooses. The client would like deferred compensation because it enables him or her to increase their long-term savings in a tax-efficient manner. Interestingly, while the IRS does not like deferred compensation arrangements where the benefactor is the majority stockholder in the corporation, the Tax Court has upheld the arrangement when it was carefully structured.[5]

Obviously, tax planning, in spite of its relatively modest Wealth Management Index score, has tremendous ramifications. A dollar given to the government has a return that is far more patriotic than wealth enhancing. Tax planning strategies can be covered annually and scoring will be maximized through the discussion around these ideas. Almost all the planning involves shades of gray rather than blacks and whites. Clients must choose their own color chart.

Summary

The income planning area covers a wide variety of topics that are instrumental in the development and monitoring of a successful financial plan. This may be the most difficult area to score for Wealth Management Index purposes because of the many

---

[5] *Casale* v. *Commissioner*, 247 F. 2d 440 (2nd Cir. 1957).

permutations that people have with their budgets and tax choices. The key is to do exhaustive work on the topics so that consequences of actions can be fully understood.

CASE STUDY

FACTS

Mr. and Mrs. Case own a software development firm. They started the business 5 years ago and have developed applications that are now standard with the shipment of IBM machines. They have been able to keep their operation small. They have no other staff.

Their IBM contract pays them $100,000 a quarter. Additionally, they have the right to license the product to other operators or end-users. While the IBM contract is secure, the Cases are in an industry where change is rapid and endemic. It is therefore difficult to project revenues beyond 3 years.

The Cases are young and healthy. They were both software engineers prior to starting the company. They have one young child and would like to have another one.

The areas of disability and income protection for the Wealth Management Index follow:

1. Do you have too much or too little disability protection given your assets and income and will it pay you should you be unable to work?
   - What are the Cases' income needs?
   - What self-funding capabilities do they have?
   - How can we implement the plan?
2. Did you receive in income from all sources what you expected to?
   - What will the Cases receive from IBM and any other contracts they may have?
   - What type of control do they have over the timing of their income?
3. Did you spend according to plan?
   - How have the Cases tracked their spending?

4. Did you use all reasonable means to reduce your taxes?

- What marginal federal tax bracket are the Cases in and what is their opportunity to straddle brackets?
- Do the Cases have appropriate retirement plans and benefit programs?
- What asset transference concepts are appropriate?

SCORING FOR THE WEALTH MANAGEMENT INDEX

Disability Insurance

The Cases have a product that they sell. This makes most of their new responsibilities research and development. This makes disability planning interesting. The Cases owned personal disability coverage purchased when they were software engineers. In working through the Wealth Management Index, it was discovered that while this coverage had an own-occupation definition for disability, it also required a loss of time and of earnings. The Cases' income stream will continue for some time, though, because of the contract on their software.

We received written notification from the insurance carrier that if a disability occurred, dropping the injured Case from the payroll would help only to the extent that there were not extensive dividends paid from the company. If we just had the healthy spouse draw more income, then a much larger percentage of the working spouse's income would be subjected to Medicare tax. It was decided to take out new policies that had more liberal definitions of disability.

Since their income stream is predictable (at least over the short term), we were most concerned with extended disability. Therefore, to save premiums, we extended the waiting period on Mr. Case. We kept Mrs. Case's waiting period shorter, in case she has a problem pregnancy.

We also purchased business-overhead policies as well as a buy-out policy for their buy/sells.

The Cases qualify for the maximum 8 points here $(100 \times (.2 \times .4))$.

Income Analysis

Understanding the Cases' income stream is pretty easy since almost all of their revenues come from the IBM contract. They do have some capability to perform end-of-the-year planning because they are cash-basis taxpayers. This will be most helpful in the last year of their IBM contract.

Again, the Cases earn the maximum for this category, 4 points (100 × (.2 × .4)).

Spending

The Cases feel that they save as much as they can so were uninterested in a detailed analysis of this area. Based on the numbers that they gave us for a budget, there was almost $30,000 of slippage (a little more than 7 percent of their income). We went over the possibility of setting up a banking relationship and a credit card that would make it very easy to follow their spending. They realized that this would be a good idea, but did not currently want to be constrained. They will reconsider this next year.

The Cases earn zero points here (100 × {(.2 × .2) × 0}).

Tax Planning

The Cases are in the highest marginal federal tax bracket. Their contract will keep them there, unless tax rates change. This makes short-term deferral less meaningful. The tax analysis earns them 1.2 points (100 × {(.2 × .2) × .3}).

On the other hand, the Cases have established a pension/profit-sharing plan into which they are funding $30,000 each. They are keeping their salaries at a level that enables them to maximize the pension and profit sharing and dividending out the rest of their income. This saves them on Medicare taxes.

Their health insurance is only 25 percent deductible because of their S-corp status. They have decided not to move to a C-corp. Their youngest child is in school, not daycare.

Give the Cases another 1.2 points.

There is no stock option planning at this point, so we credit the .8 points to them (100 × {(.2 × .2) × .2}).

They wish to maintain control of their assets so they did not wish to set up an UTMA for their child. They were also uncomfortable with establishing a minor's trust until their daughter gets older. However, they are not opposed to having the child perform some work for them when she is of a reasonable age to do so. We wished to gift some appreciated stock to charity for their gifts this year but did not receive the paperwork back in time to consummate the transaction. This caused a modest reduction in scoring. Otherwise, we explored this area reasonably well and made conscious decisions to defer or not.

They score .6 points here $(100 \times \{(.2 \times .2) \times (.2 \times .75)\})$. The .75 reflects a 25 percent reduction in the transference category for the failed charitable bequest.

SUMMARY

The Cases earned 15.8 out of a possible 20 points. While they did relatively well from a scoring standpoint, the rejection of the budget could prove to be an ongoing stumbling block. It will clearly become more important to them if their income drops.

This area will most likely change in the next few years due to the birth of another child, transfer measures for the older child, more employees, and an inevitable loss of the IBM contract. Regular review will anticipate and allow for these changes with the least amount of financial disruption possible.

6

DEBT MANAGEMENT (LEVERAGE)

Debt management is an important component of all financial planning. Regardless of the amount of money that a client has, the decisions regarding what is an appropriate amount of borrowing must be conscious. This determination of reasonableness is what will enable the client to maximize points in this area of the Wealth Management Index.

Percent of Index (10%) for Debt Management (Leverage)

	Percent of Debt Management Scale	Total Index Weight
Have you access to as much debt as reasonably possible and at the best available rates?	30%	3%
Is your current ratio better than 2:1 and is your total debt reasonable as a percentage of assets?	40	4
Have you managed your debt as expected?	20	2
Is your debt tax-efficient?	10	1

Have You Access to as Much Debt as Reasonably Possible and at the Best Available Rates?

Debt is a useful financial planning tool when used properly. It is a tremendous nemesis to overall wealth building if used incorrectly. Available debt can serve as an emergency fund, it can provide flexibility when making timing decisions for tax purposes, and it can provide some security should disaster strike. For these reasons, it makes sense to avail clients of the most inexpensive or no-cost credit that they can obtain. Clients who abhor debt should still attempt to set up a no-cost home equity line of credit up to the maximum limits. While they may choose never to access this line, the problem with credit is that while it is easy to get when you don't need it, it is way too difficult to get when you do.

Couple this home equity debt with the maximum unsecured lines of credit obtainable. While preference should be to use the deductible (although secured) debt, the unsecured line enables some clients to front business start-up costs that they would otherwise have been unable to finance because of little or no track records.

Credit cards are also sources of free financing. Many cards offer no annual fee and surprisingly large credit limits. These can be unusually important vehicles for increasing flexibility. For example, we had a client who was able to "purchase" a foreclosed property from a bank for $185,000, a drastically reduced price. He was simultaneously selling it for $215,000. Theoretically, he would make $30,000 and never have put up any money.

Unfortunately, his buyer's financing was delayed 1 month. Because our client had some cash, a large home equity line, some margin availability, and unused credit cards, he was able to finance this transaction for 30 days until the deal closed. Everything happened so quickly that he would have been unable to obtain a mortgage himself; this available credit let him pocket over $28,000 after interest costs.

If the sale had fallen through, the client would have taken out a no-cost adjustable rate mortgage to clean up his outstanding balances until the house was sold. This was as close to a riskless transaction that you can come across, only made possible because of a preplanned, effective debt strategy. While the client may have been lucky to have this opportunity surface, the adage that "luck is when preparation meets opportunity" certainly held true here.

The starting point for debt management, therefore, is a thorough review of all current areas of debt as well as an evaluation of areas of potentially available credit. From this evaluation, you can begin to develop sensible goals to gauge success.

Interest Rates   Shopping the loan rates available to a client is another valuable benefit of the Wealth Management Index. Since in your service you are looking at the client's total picture, mortgage and home equity interest can provide tremendous planning opportunities.

For example, if you have a client who will almost certainly be moving due to an occupation change, marriage, or personal goal within a 3-year period, regular no-cost refinancings on adjustable rate mortgages can provide constantly improving cash flow with not much downside risk. The opportunity for participating in even modest interest rate drops with no concomitant increase in the total indebtedness is a tremendous benefit.

As a planner you may have immense leverage in the ability to get the best possible interest rates for your client. The fact that you have excellent and organized information, your ability to provide cash flows and balance sheets, and your regular monitoring of investments provides great comfort to many bankers. This amount of information coupled with the number of potential clients you can provide a bank does give you bargaining power on your clients' behalf. We have been able to regularly reduce clients' home equity interest rates from two over prime to as low as prime (sometimes even lower).

The banking relationship is one of the most important bonds that you can provide to your client. Many clients have a tremendous amount of apprehension with banks, mostly because they don't have the mind set that the bank is there to serve them. By establishing a relationship where your client allows you to freely exchange information with his or her banker, you set up a synergistic relationship that the client truly values. The bankers we use will call us to let us know if the client seems to be carrying excessive balances in their savings or checking accounts. This kind of regular and consistent information is necessary for providing comprehensive wealth management.

Is Your Current Ratio Better Than 2:1 and Is Your Total Debt Reasonable as a Percentage of Your Assets?

To get a handle on debt management, you must first produce a balance sheet for the client. The balance sheet will provide the focus for those items in most need of attention. The strength of a client's financial position can first be measured by the current ratio. This is simply the value of the client's short-term assets (those items that can reasonably quickly be turned into cash) divided by the client's short-term liabilities (those debts that are due within a year).

The current ratio for a client should be at least 2:1. The client should have at least twice as many marketable assets as short-term debts. This obvious statement does not always reflect the client's original wishes. It is not infrequent that clients want to begin investing before they have paid off their short-term debt. The investment account merely has a placebo security effect; clients are probably worse off with investments equal to their short-term debt than they would be with no investments and no debt.

Clients probably have more current assets than they imagine. Cash value of life insurance can provide immediate liquidity yet is often overlooked in determining this ratio.

I don't use the current ratio in the pure accounting sense. Stock mutual funds are marketable and not liquid so their value could change overnight. In spite of this, we view these dollars as easily accessible and therefore current. The risk associated with factoring those investments in the calculation of the current ratio is outweighed by the flexibility the inclusion gives the client as to making choices relative to the size of emergency funds and the effective use of margin loans. On the other hand, items such as limited partnerships should not be considered in the calculation of the current ratio. Even though there is a secondary market for some partnerships, it is so inefficient that a premature sale would be too costly to justify.

Debt Level   The current ratio is a tool to measure the relative liquidity of a client. A client will probably have significantly greater overall debt than short-term debt. It is necessary to benchmark an appropriate level of overall debt.

Planners will argue this area forever. There is nothing more subjective than what is a reasonable level of overall debt. We can try to justify large mortgages by their somewhat tax deductible nature. We can talk about how so much of the great wealth in this world is as a result of leverage. Using a business model as a yardstick, the use of ratios to predict bankruptcy and to measure profitability, liquidity, and solvency have prevailed as significant indicators of progress over time and as standards for comparison of similar companies within an industry.[1] Banks have

---

[1] Sharon A. DeVaney and Ruth H. Lytton, "Household Insolvency: A Review of Household Debt Repayment, Delinquency, and Bankruptcy," *Financial Services Review* 4, no. 2, 1995.

been using ratios to determine business solvency for years. Unfortunately, the use of ratios on the personal side has been undeveloped. Griffith has come up with 16 ratios that can be used to assess personal financial statements. Prather has somewhat modified them as follows:

Liquidity

- Liquid assets/monthly expenses.
- Liquid and financial assets/monthly expenses.

Debt

- Liquid assets/total debt.
- Liquid and financial assets/debt.
- Liquid assets/nonmortgage debt.
- Liquid assets/1-year debt payment.
- Liquid and financial assets/1-year debt payment.

Inflation Protection

- Tangible and equity assets/fixed-dollar assets.

Derivatives of Net Worth

- Tangible and equity less home/net worth.
- Nonmortgage debt/net worth.
- Debt/asset.
- Liquid assets/total assets.
- Liquid and financial assets/total assets.

- ◆ Tangible and equity assets/total assets.
- ◆ Tangible assets/total assets.
- ◆ Income-generating assets/total assets.[2]

Most of us do not use ratios at all or at best very little. As a result, there is little against which to make assessments. Pragmatically, absent standard measurements, you and your client should reach conclusions regarding these ratios. The client will turn to you for guidance; the client must ultimately determine the comfort level.

I am often ill at ease with what I advise my clients regarding an appropriate level of indebtedness. I personally do not care for debt, which could be a bias developed from struggling as a self-employed financial planner for my first few years until I was able to build my practice. I hope that I am careful not to project my bias too strongly, although I will admit that many of our clients are paying off their mortgages more rapidly than the regular amortization schedules call for. But I believe that there is a line that clients must walk so that they do not pay down debt to the exclusion of investing.

It seems that when confronted with the choice, most clients (greedy clients aside) resonate with the thought of being completely unencumbered by debt and the freedom that they perceive it may bring them. Quite honestly, over the 1980s the paydown of debt weighed against the gains in the stock market would have been like a feather weighed against a rock. On the other hand, those clients who were able to both pay down their debt and invest reasonable amounts do not regret their choice. Conversely, in the 1970s, clients who invested solely at the expense of debt don't feel so good about that choice.

---

[2] Ibid.

We are familiar with the concept of marginal utility from basic economics. Utility (satisfaction) for a product does not move in a straight line. At some point, we will be satiated with satisfaction from an abundance of a product and our satisfaction may actually diminish. In investments, above some level, additional incremental returns to the client do not provide as much utility as the disutility suffered from incremental losses.

The mathematician Daniel Bernoulli in his treatise *Exposition of a New Theory on the Measurement of Risk,* published in 1738, pointed out that the determination of the value of an item must not be based on price, but rather on the utility it yields."[3] This is also how we should view the reduction of debt. While there may be financial reasons for investing rather than paying down debt, this does not override the issue of a client's overall satisfaction with a strategy. This is especially true in this area because outcomes are not even close to certain.

Have You Managed Your Debt as Expected?

Managing debt as planned involves understanding what plans your client has for going into debt and managing to those plans. It also involves trying to help the client to be released from any guarantees for which he or she may no longer need to provide.

Some of our clients have been forced to guarantee their debt with more than the assets specific to the debt. These personal guarantees are especially prevalent for business owners or professionals. For businesses or professional associations, you may be working with only one of the partners. The personal guarantees that your client provides can be very expensive if one of the other partners runs into financial difficulties.

---

[3] Peter Bernstein, *The Portable MBA in Investment* (New York: John Wiley & Sons, 1995), p. 37.

Most personal guarantees are written by the banks as joint and several. This means that any individual partner is responsible for the full amount of the loan, regardless of whether he or she is meeting the payments accordingly. This puts the client at undue risk.

If you cannot get the personal guarantees lifted (and this should be attempted every year), then you should at least try to change the responsibility of the debt from joint and several to a percentage basis. If the client is a 25 percent owner of the partnership, then he or she can be responsible for 25 percent of the debt.

While this is reasonable in theory, it does not go quite so smoothly in practice. The fact that your client has a strong balance sheet is the reason that the joint and several guarantee is so compelling to the banker. Not all partners have equal financial conditions, so the more people the banker can tie up, the better the security on the note. The inducement for the bank to lift the personal guarantees, especially on loans that have been operating for some time, is the intangible notion of customer service combined with the pragmatism in preempting the client from shopping the loan elsewhere. If you develop a portfolio of banks with which you are operating, you will be surprised at your ability to negotiate the removal of these guarantees.

Another area of debt management includes purchase timing. There may be occasions where temporarily going into debt as a method of maximizing dollars is useful. We had a client who leased a car for her use prior to working with us. She was a physician and gained no tax advantages from leasing. The lease was expiring and she wanted to buy a different car, but she wanted to wait until the new models came out. Rather than rewrite the lease for an additional 6 months, we purchased the car off the lease, drove it until the new models came out, and then traded it in on a new model. We were able to save the client a few thousand dollars between new lease costs associated with this type of financing, the price differential between the trade-in value and the purchase price off lease, and the spread between the home equity debt used for the outright purchase versus the nondeductible lease rate. Ideally, we will eventually get the client in queue to pay cash for her cars, but getting her off lease was a good start.

Is Your Debt Tax-Efficient?

If a client is going to actually use debt, then the tax efficiency of the loans need to be assessed. This can be an area where poor planning could be quite costly to the client. There are several categories of interest expense. Generally, there is a tracing of the interest to one of these categories to determine deductibility:

1. *Trade or business interest.* This interest is almost always fully deductible against any income.

2. *Passive activity interest.* This interest is only deductible to the extent of passive activity income or after the disposition of that passive activity business.

3. *Investment interest.* This can be deducted up to the extent of investment income. Unused deductions here can be carried forward.

4. *Interest attributable to tax-deferred payments.* This allows a deduction for the interest that estates pay on deferred estate taxes.

5. *Consumer interest.* This is the catchall. All interest not covered in one of the other categories is consumer interest and not deductible.

6. *Qualified residence interest.* Tracing rules do not apply here. All acquisition indebtedness up to $1 million is deductible here. This acquisition indebted-

ness is reduced by each principal payment made. You can also deduct interest on up to $100,000 of home equity interest and even go beyond that if the loan is for excess medical or educational costs.[4]

Because of the tracing regulations, it is the use of the proceeds that determines what category of loan it is. This means that you can't deduct your margin interest for the purchase of a car.

There are certain items that are clearly deductible, but due to the Tax Reform Act of 1986 are subjected to phase-out restrictions. Acquisition indebtedness to finance a first or second home or its improvements is deductible but is subjected to phaseouts. Home equity loans over $100,000 are also deductible but are also subjected to phaseouts.

In most cases, it makes sense to move debt that is not currently deductible into a deductible home equity loan, but there are important caveats. For example, car companies often offer very low interest loans that may be worth continuing. On the other hand, don't be lured by these loans merely because they are low interest. The cost of the lower interest rate could be tacked onto the minimum price of the car. Separate out the car purchase from the financing.

Older student loans are also often low interest. They also often extend for many years. An evaluation of the cost of the loan versus the flexibility of low (albeit nondeductible) payments must be integrated into the rest of the plan.

There is no doubt that a home equity loan, while deductible, also increases the default risk on what is typically the client's most sacred asset. Some clients may be very uncomfortable with

---

[4] PlainTalk, "Avoiding the Interest Traps," Program 91 (Fall City, WA: Planning Focus, Inc., 1994).

the security sacrifice for the deductibility gain. The security sacrifice is somewhat illusory, though. Most clients will not run into the kind of trouble where their home is in jeopardy; trying to convince those with that concern otherwise, though, is probably unproductive.

The tracing rules make it important to be careful how you structure transactions. It is perfectly all right to set up a margin loan to buy additional stock and pay cash for the car you are about to purchase. It is even allowable to pay cash for the car, then take out a loan using the car as collateral, and then invest the loan into the stock market, thereby making the interest on the loan investment interest. It could come into question if you borrowed from the margin account and then made a car purchase. Interestingly, if the client borrowed $20,000 to buy a car and $20,000 to buy stock, the car would be consumer interest and the stock would be investment interest. If the client borrowed one $40,000 amount, all interest payments would be consumer interest until the car is paid off. This means that the client would be generating a constant level of investment interest.[5]

Summary

Appropriate debt management does not involve black box analysis. It is weighing the client's expressed objectives against his or her actions combined with choosing between the "best" financial moves versus the client's level of comfort. This area of the Wealth Management Index is one that needs constant adjusting and negotiating. This area also is one that can't be dismissed merely because of discomfort in discussing with clients their conflict between what they say and what they do.

---

[5] Ibid.

A good score in the debt management component of the Wealth Management Index will mean that your client has an understanding of his or her spending and saving patterns and will help you determine at a core level whether the client is living beyond his or her means. It is the control over these patterns that will enhance your performance on the asset management side by allowing you to be more growth oriented. Inappropriate debt creates an obstacle to growth because of excess carrying costs and a weak balance sheet which must be improved. Managing debt then will ultimately allow your client to accept short-term volatility.

CASE STUDY

FACTS

Jerry and Mary Reynolds are both young physicians. Jerry just completed his fellowship in radiation oncology and Mary has been in family practice for the last 3 years.

They have three young children. Mary currently makes $125,000 a year and does not anticipate her salary increasing by more than inflation. Jerry has joined a group and has a graduated salary structure of $175,000 in year 1, $235,000 in year 2, $325,000 in year 3, and full partnership in the year 4. Partners currently earn $500,000. As a partner, Jerry will also have the opportunity to invest in additional practices that are being developed in rural areas.

Jerry and Mary have a $90,000, 8.25 percent 30-year fixed rate mortgage on a house valued at $130,000, and student loans that total $70,000 and are mostly at 9 percent interest. Other than a 401(k) for Mary (which she is fully funding) and personal property, they have no other assets.

Jerry and Mary would like to get into their $600,000 dream house within 1 year. They would also like to begin saving for their children's education. They wish to buy Jerry a new $30,000 van this year.

They believe that they can live entirely off Jerry's salary as they save for their home.

As we work through the debt planning area of the Wealth Management Index for this year, we will cover the following areas:

1. Is your current ratio stronger than 2:1 and is your total debt reasonable as a percentage of your total assets?
   ◆ How is the current ratio for the Reynolds?
   ◆ What is a reasonable debt structure for them?
2. Is your debt tax-efficient?
3. Have you access to as much debt as reasonably possible and at the best available rates?
   ◆ What is the type of credit available for the Reynolds?
   ◆ What rates are appropriate on this credit?
4. Is the debt managed appropriately?

SCORING FOR THE WEALTH MANAGEMENT INDEX

Current Ratio and Total Debt

Short-term debt was not an issue for the Reynolds. It was more important to focus on the rest of their debt structure.

The Reynolds' objectives may have seemed at cross purposes. On the one hand, there was expensive student loan debt that was both long term and nondeductible. We also had this dream of buying the $600,000 home. To avoid some of the extra costs in mortgage financing, we were hoping to put 20 percent down.

By delaying the home purchase until the end of the year, we could have more time to build up reserves or pay down other debt.

First, we set the Reynolds up with a banking relationship at a bank where we had a tremendous amount of leverage (because of other successful clients that we brought there). We were uncertain what we would need from the bank or when we would need it, but we knew we wanted the relationship to be nimble.

We then refinanced their current home with a zero-cost adjustable rate mortgage at 6.75 percent. We were planning on moving the Reynolds before the mortgage would adjust up. The difference in the mortgage interest rates created around $1,800 of before-tax savings.

We then aggressively saved Mary's paycheck into this new mortgage. This served two purposes. It effectively allowed us to earn 6.75 percent on very short-term money and protected us at adjustment time should the Reynolds not move by then. The Reynolds also had stated unequivocally that they would not buy a new home until this one sold. By the end of the year, we had approximately $100,000 of home equity built up.

In spite of the fact that the Reynolds actually began the year with a negative net worth, their debt structure did not seem too great for their incomes. The investment into the education of both of them is finally generating significant returns.

Give the Reynolds all 4 points in this area $(100 \times (.1 \times .4))$.

Debt Management

We chose not to pay off the student loans until after we'd saved the 20 percent down payment for the new home. The bank allowed us to borrow $20,000 unsecured to get us to the needed down payment level.

Once we closed on the house, we applied for a $100,000 home equity loan. We used this to pay off the unsecured credit line and the student loans.

During the next year, we will continue to reduce the home equity line, set aside some money for furnishings, and begin a general savings program.

The Reynolds earn a full 2 points for debt management $(100 \times (.1 \times .2))$.

Tax Efficiency

The debt of the Reynolds did not become tax-efficient until the new home was bought and the new home equity line was established. This was a conscious choice, though. Since the year ended with all debt being fully deductible, they receive 1 point $(100 \times (.1 \times .1))$.

Accessing Debt

This was a good category for the Reynolds. When they first came in, we established a $40,000 line on their old home. We also set up a ready reserve on their checking account that totaled $20,000 and an additional unsecured line for $50,000 (which we used for the down payment). All of these were at one-half of 1 percent over prime.

We also worked with the bank to obtain lines of credit tied directly to the investment in the clinics as Jerry becomes eligible to participate. The cash flow from these is ample enough to service the debt and pay down the notes. We are trying to make the debt service deductible as investment interest.

Again, give the Reynolds the full 3 points ($100 \times (.1 \times .3)$).

SUMMARY

The Reynolds earned all 10 points here. You can see how effectively creating and managing debt can be a tremendous lever for helping people reach their objectives. Given the significant income level that the couple has and also their inclination to live off only one income, even if Jerry's income never reaches expected levels at the partnership, the Reynolds can still live their dream.

CHAPTER

7

INVESTMENT PLANNING (ACCUMULATION)

While investment planning seems to be the area about which clients are almost always most concerned and most interested, it is this very focus that makes them lose sight of the myriad of planning issues confronting them on their path to wealth accumulation and preservation.

The importance of accumulation planning is represented by its high relative score in the Wealth Management Index. Investment planning represents 25 percent of the total of the index, more than any individual category other than asset protection. Some people may argue that it should represent more than this. On a relative value scale, it does not make sense to de-emphasize any other items for increased importance in this area.

Asset protection is the assurance that all you have accumulated will be there. Does it matter what rate of return clients receive on their investments if they have to turn them over to a creditor after losing a judgment?

Income protection is the assurance that the client will live the lifestyle he or she desires. For most clients, can you honestly say that they would accept the Faustian choice of another

1 percent on their investment portfolio in return for giving up their ability to work?

Debt management is the assurance that clients are not over-burdened by their cost of funds and that they have structured their loans to, wherever possible, relieve them of personal liability. The importance of this was magnified during the halcyon days of private partnerships with recourse debt, sometimes turning wealthy people into paupers seemingly overnight.

Estate planning is the assurance that what clients have built will be distributed to whomever or whatever they desire. Granted, if the assets have not grown at a reasonable rate, the distribution figures are less important, but a 55 percent estate tax rate constitutes over 4 years of historical growth in small caps. It seems both inconsistent and imprudent to build without an eye toward preservation.

Don't allow the popularity or complexity of, or your expertise in, investment planning to give it an exaggerated sense of importance in the context of total wealth management. While the process around growing a client's assets is essential to wealth management, it is not necessarily the essence of wealth management.

Percent of Index (25%) for Investment Planning (Accumulation)

	Percent of Investment Planning Scale	Total Index Weight
Is your asset allocation appropriate?	40%	10%
How did your actual rate of return compare with the expected rate (CPI plus target percentage)?	10	2.5
Were your annual contributions or withdrawals at target?	40	10
Was the portfolio income tax-efficient?	5	1.25
Have you set aside enough cash for purchases to be made in the next 3 years?	5	1.25

Is Your Asset Allocation Appropriate?

If everything related to investment planning is based on the client's stated objectives, then it stands to reason that the asset allocation for that client must be consistent with those objectives. This makes the asset allocation decision 40 percent of the value of the whole investment planning conundrum. (I use the word conundrum consciously. It is in stark contrast to the black box that our clients often wish us to have).

One of the most-used resources for the asset allocation discussion is a study performed by Gary Brinson and his peers. The study involved 91 pension plans between 1974 and 1983 and found that, on average, 93.6 percent of the variation of total returns came from asset allocation decisions over stock selection or timing decisions.[1] Although I find the magnitude of the Brinson et al study somewhat counterintuitive, I concede that a significant portion of investment performance is asset allocation driven. Clearly the allocation decision is a key component to effective wealth management.

The benchmark for long-term wealth management should not be a stock or bond index, but rather the Consumer Price Index (technically, it should be the client's price index as determined by what the client spends money on) plus an incremental return. Comparing returns against other indexes is informative, but not necessarily useful. By its very nature, an asset allocation strategy is a risk-control strategy. Should this type of portfolio's returns exceed common-growth stock market returns it is because of cyclicality, not prescience. On the other hand, growing client buying power is a key ingredient for overall wealth management.

---

[1] Gary P. Brinson, L. Randolph Hood, and Gilbert L. Beebower, "Determinants of Portfolio Performance," *Financial Analysts Journal*, July–August 1986, pp. 39–44.

The incremental return added to the CPI is the investment policy return. It should be based on long-term, historical trends. The Ibbotson work on asset class returns from 1925 to the present provides an excellent launching pad for crafting policy returns.[2] By developing combinations of long-term stock and bond performance and by weaving in international stocks and bonds through either optimization programs or formulation, you can establish expected portfolio returns above the CPI with some comfort (at least one standard deviation's worth).

It is disturbing to hear people talk of only nominal returns and to then extrapolate recent success into long-term expectations. Comparing returns against the CPI plus your hurdle presents a voice of reason during the stampede to grab last year's top performers. This perspective refocuses attention on total wealth over time. Mark Balasa of the Burton Group in Schaumberg, Illinois, illustrates this point beautifully on his client reporting. His colorful line graph shows three since-inception returns: Client actual return, client policy return, and the CPI.

It is also appropriate, though, to display how the mutual funds or stocks that you have selected with the client have done relative to their respective benchmarks. Unless you are using only index funds, this is not as easy as it may seem. Style drift, where a mutual fund that was successful owning one type of stock changes its selection criteria but does not note this, or tracking error, where a fund does not match what it sets out to do, makes comparisons against benchmarks somewhat suspect. Attribution analysis, a study of how much of a fund's return comes from a particular style, is really in its infancy and is both expensive to monitor and not necessarily accurate. Ideally, the mutual fund industry will be more responsive to our profession

---

[2] Roger G. Ibbotson and Rex A. Sinquefield, *Stocks, Bonds, Bills, and Inflation* (SBGI), (Chicago: Ibbotson Associates), updated annually.

and will begin revealing their portfolios in a timely manner; until then, we need to try to work around them.

How one manages this in the meantime, then, is based upon the planner's biases coupled with the client's expectations. If a planner believes in stock selection, he or she will most likely convince clients of this and will ultimately develop portfolios where style drift and benchmark returns will need to be regularly reviewed. If a planner is an indexer, style drift and tracking errors are not very big concerns.

Most of our clients seem to want individual managers rather than all index funds but, frankly, I am not sure if it is because I prefer managers or because they do. I do believe that there is a place for the passionate investor, but I also think that this place is shrinking during this high-tech information-centered era. It is appearing more and more difficult to beat the markets.

Annual contributions are valued in the Wealth Management Index as importantly as the asset allocation decision. If a client is overspending and therefore not contributing to the plan at the level suggested or is removing more money out of the plan than anticipated, it could be very difficult to meet objectives. While with extremely large portfolios where the client has no danger of outliving his or her assets this may seem trivial, it still is a very useful tool in determining whether the client is living his or her expressed values. To de-emphasize this component is to disregard what the client has the most direct control over. It may point to other inconsistencies in the plan that will manifest themselves in more subtle, and potentially pernicious, ways.

The tax efficiency of the portfolio represents a relatively small piece of the total index. Tax decisions should not take precedent over investment decisions, although they need to be considered within the investment decisions. Tax efficiency can often be a smoke screen. It is bandied about by proponents of managed individual stock portfolios where theoretically the manager has control over the timing of the sell decisions versus managed mutual fund portfolios, where the investor is "invisible" to the manager. While it is true that there is more control over distributions within a stock account versus a fund account, as later described, there are also some things you can do to manage the mutual funds more tax-efficiently.

Encouraging clients to set aside cash during the raging bull market of the 1980s and early 1990s was a lot like encouraging Pharaoh to set aside crops prior to the drought. Realistically, clients should not be invested if they intend to spend the money within a 3-year time frame. If the market were to correct, there may not be adequate time to recover losses. Even on accounts that are using a payout ratio (where a client withdraws a specific percentage from the portfolio), setting aside the cash for the first year is a good idea. Making this isolated in the Wealth Management Index, even at such a nominal level, underscores the importance of time horizon with wealth management.

Investment Policy   The asset allocation decision must be part of the investment policy. To blindly allocate via optimization without first establishing an investment policy would be like selling a beautiful silk sport coat to an aborigine—the coat might be beautiful, but it won't wear very well.

Establishing an investment policy involves developing an understanding of the client's personality as well as financial situation. The investment policy is the tool from which you will measure the appropriateness of all investment decisions. The appropriateness will not be measured by rate of return but by the alignment with the overall expectations jointly established with your client and the understanding of the probability of achieving those expectations. Investment policy guru Charles Ellis says, "Clients own the central responsibility for formulating and assuring implementation of a long-term investment policy. . . . the responsibility cannot be delegated to investment managers."[3]

There are several items around which you must gather your arms to launch the investment policy. Don Trone and William Allbright in their book *Procedural Prudence* point to "four key variables (that) enter into every asset allocation decision: (1) time horizon of the portfolio; (2) assumed risk tolerance or variability of returns; (3) expected rate of return; (4) selection of asset classes."[4] By gaining an understanding of and consensus on these key areas you can then construct a suitable model for your client.

Virtually all foundations and pension plans have written investment policies around which their investment decisions are made. The investment policy creates a discipline and delivers parameters with which to make suitable investment decisions. There is no reason why individual clients should not also use this tool in appropriating their dollars.

A personal investment policy needs to include many of the same items that an institutional investment policy harbors. It is especially important in individual investment policies to understand things such as time horizon before expected withdrawals will occur as well as expected annual contributions. These two pieces of information will aid you in helping the client make prudent asset allocation decisions and will take away some of the natural tendency to try to time the market.

A portfolio that will have regular contributions is already utilizing dollar cost averaging to some extent. These additions,

---

[3] Charles D. Ellis, *Investment Policy* (Burr Ridge, IL: Irwin Professional Publishing, 1985), p. 3.

[4] Donald B. Trone and William R. Allbright, *Procedural Prudence* (Cincinnati, OH: Veale and Associates), p. 15.

coupled with a reasonable time horizon, allow for the client to be more invested than what he or she may otherwise choose. Obviously, the importance of the contributions is related to the size of the portfolio.

The investment policy also establishes liquidity versus marketability needs for the portfolio. It should state the percentage of the portfolio that is allowed to be invested in investments that may not be readily marketable, such as limited partnerships or venture capital. If nonmarketable instruments are going to be proposed, then this piece of the investment policy must be very carefully considered. While the rest of the policy could be easily (although possibly expensively) adapted to reflect significant changes in a client's situation, nonmarketable instruments afford no such luxury. Many of us who have been in business for several years can commiserate about the angst that this can cause an unprepared client.

Expected returns *over a reasonable time horizon* are also integral in a well-crafted investment policy. It is over these expected returns that you must be willing to lose the greedy client. For most of our individual clients, expected returns should be measured against either their personal inflation rate or the CPI. Most people should be surprised at how low those expected returns are. In recent years, the extraordinary growth of the stock market has caused a spate of investment amnesia that is violent in its proportion. Salvador Dali said, "The difference between false memories and true ones is the same as for jewels: it is always the false ones that look the most real, the most brilliant."[5] This is unfortunately the case with the recent (less than 15-year) dramatic ascendance of stocks, which has caused the long-term performance of stocks to pale in comparison.

---

[5] Salvador Dali, *The Secret Life of Salvador Dali*. Translated by Haakon Chevalier. (New York: Dover, 1993).

The expected return will focus the client back to personal objectives rather than on the uncertainties of the capital markets. When talking about returns, I also like the conclusion drawn by Charles Ellis in his book *Investment Policy*. He mentions that Peter Bernstein said, "Investors like best those market movements that are most adverse to their long- term interests, and most dislike market movements that are, in fact, in their long-term interests."[6] The long-term investor is a net buyer of stocks and therefore continues to get to add to portfolio when the market is downtrodden. The only investor who needs to care about whether the market is increasing is one who is ultimately disposing of his or her portfolio. While this is true in theory, if our clients are having annual "market correction" parties, rest assured that it won't be long before we no longer make the guest list. If the expected return numbers are reasonable and historical, your relationship as an asset manager is more easily cemented.

It is also important to distinguish who is making the final decisions when it comes to investment selection. Since my firm does not exercise discretion over our clients' assets, we are clear to state in the investment policy that the client is ultimately responsible for the investment decisions. I don't believe that this changes our capacity as fiduciaries, but it does underscore the interdependent relationship we have with our client.

I am not in favor of extensive investment policies for most individuals. While these abbreviated investment policies don't necessarily provide the detail that institutional policies must, if the salient points are covered in a reasonable manner, the document is a more useful working one. I know that some would argue this point, but again it speaks to pragmatism over perfection.

---

[6] Charles D. Ellis, *Investment Policy* (Burr Ridge, IL: Irwin Professional Publishing, 1985), p. 54.

Ultimately, our clients must be as responsible for the policy as we are. If the key areas are covered in the investment policy, there is a higher likelihood that the client will be more involved with it. I can only provide anecdotal evidence of this—have you fully read your credit card agreements or property/casualty policy?

Interestingly, even the "abbreviated" investment policy should give the information needed to annually assess all parts of the accumulation section of the Wealth Management Index. This policy will still cover the asset allocation, the rate-of-return expectations as compared with the CPI, and the expected annual contributions or withdrawals. The need for tax efficiency will be discussed, as should a disclaimer statement mentioning appropriate levels of cash to be held outside the investment account.

How Did Your Actual Rate of Return Compare with the Expected Rate (CPI Plus Target Percentage)?

Market timing is impossible. Reams of research supports this. Yet over and over our greedy clients expect us to be fully invested in good markets and completely in cash in bad. Now we also have to be in the correct good market.

Market timing is most unattractive because reasonably short periods provide inordinately large rates of return. It is almost impossible to know when those periods will begin and it is extremely costly not to be invested when they start. For example, "removing just 10 days from the 9 years dating from 1982–1990 (a total of 2,250 trading days)—less than .5 percent of the total period—would reduce the investor's average annual rate of return by one-third (from 18 to 12 percent).[7]

---

[7] Peter L. Bernstein, *The Portable MBA in Investment* (New York: John Wiley & Sons, 1995).

Also, since we have already established that to be an investor you must by definition have a long-term time horizon, the client's risk is not being in the market for the next 20 percent correction but being out of the market for the next 100 percent increase.

It is not in my purview to write a tome on the fallacy of market timing. Roger Gibson's book *Asset Allocation* gives much supporting research to help dispel the market timing myth.[8] Harold Evensky's seminal book on wealth management also speaks to the problems with market timing.[9] It is useful to become acquainted with their work. I really am speaking out against broad in-and-out-of-the-market timing. Moving on the margins in the asset allocation models is market timing, but it doesn't have the same deleterious effect as broad brush decisions do.

If market timing does not work, does asset allocation do anything for the client? Absolutely. In the 1990s, it helped you to underperform a roaring US bull market because international investments and bonds invariably caused a drag on performance. So what! Your job is to attempt to help clients meet their goals and objectives as defined by them. To do this, you need to choose to sacrifice maximum returns in return for consistent returns.

Rather than stutter over this during strong US markets, continue to emphasize it. There is no reason to apologize for doing exactly what you set out to do. Don't be like the person who was afraid to meet God because he didn't know what to say if God sneezed. Your job is to continue to help clients focus on their allocations and returns as compared to the CPI.

It is apparent that if history provides us with any lessons, US stocks will outperform US company bonds over long periods of time. It would make no sense that loans to corporations to

---

[8] Roger C. Gibson, *Asset Allocation* (Burr Ridge, IL: Irwin Professional Publishing, 1990).

[9] Harold Evensky, *Wealth Management* (Burr Ridge, IL: Irwin Professional Publishing, 1996).

help them invest in their businesses would provide better returns than those very businesses over a long time horizon. For the very long-term investor, then, any bond allocation serves only to help mitigate risk as defined by short-term volatility. It certainly cannot enhance long-term returns.

Many of us presume, though, that for clients to be adequately allocated, they must have a bond component in their portfolios. For the investor with a very long time horizon, this is not the case. The coupling of bond and stock returns has been noticeable recently; more important, volatility is not the risk to the long-term investor—inflation is the risk. On the other hand (please, no one-armed economist jokes), bonds will usually help to minimize the severity of losses. For fear-based clients, this may be reason enough to use them.

Utilizing hedged foreign bonds can be an alternative to, or a partner with, US bonds. The cost of the currency hedge to the funds is minimal, yet removing the currency risk enables the foreign bond investment to be used as a portfolio stabilizer.

It is not so easy to speculate which type of stock will outperform another or which country's securities will provide the best overall returns. To try to guess this is to practice market timing. Asset allocation requires you to take some of the guesswork out of this. I say this hesitantly because I believe that there is always guesswork in investing.

No matter what we try to do, investing is a soft science, not a hard one. That means that we don't know what the future will bring for our clients. In fact, chaosticians would argue that capital markets are totally nonlinear. You must look for patterns in seemingly random events. Ironically, this very randomness is what has fueled the arguments for passive investing and efficient markets.

The asset allocation strategy must be developed with the client's goals and objectives in mind, balanced against the client's risk tolerance. The young client with a 30-year time horizon would be best suited under almost all scenarios to be 100 percent invested in stocks; if the client's risk profile does not allow him or her to stay invested and add to accounts when stocks are falling, this allocation could prove to be disastrous. We often view optimization in terms of the portfolio in a vacuum. Optimization is four-dimensional. It must include more than the risk, expected returns, and the diversification associated with investments; it must include the risk acceptance of the investor.

The asset allocation model ultimately developed will be at least partially based on expected returns. While it is almost impossible to predict returns, it makes sense to view spreads of returns among investments rather than nominal returns. For example, stocks as a performance multiple against inflation are better tools than stocks as a nominal percentage above inflation. It again focuses the client on buying power and yields a perception of volatility that is entirely different from nominal results. If inflation was 3 percent, and stocks in a given year outpaced inflation by 5 times rather than three times, it appears less dramatic than stocks outpacing inflation by 12 percent rather than 6 percent.

Part of the job of asset allocation is not only to stabilize returns, but it is also to help ground emotions. I have seen this done through a wide variety of expected returns established in developing the asset allocation model for the client. Lou Stanasolovich of Legend Financial in Pittsburgh utilizes the current CPI rate and then weaves in the historic Ibbotson numbers of various investment categories to try to display expected rates of return. Several planners use optimizers. Many planners use judgment. I think it is reasonable to use all of these methods.

Optimization is effective to the extent that the time period used for the inputs is comparable to the time period for which you are projecting. What degree of confidence do you have with markets that have gone from 80 percent individually controlled to 80 percent institutionally controlled; from the United States comprising 60 percent of the total capital markets to it comprising around 35 percent? In other words, pragmatism must rule in determining the appropriate asset mix.

By relying most heavily on the long-term historic spreads documented by Ibbotson and by broadening the available investment selection by including international stocks as a component of the equity side and hedged international bonds somewhere between the fixed income and equity side, you have the basis for the establishment of effective asset allocation decisions.

If you accept that any asset allocation model is merely a schematic theory, than you must also believe that you can try to add value by allowing this model to be somewhat dynamic (within relatively narrow confines). You can facilitate the changes by allowing for small relative changes in the allocation targets based on your empirical analysis of expected returns, or you can choose to hold hard and fast to the broad equity versus debt model and provide for some variance among categories within those models.

Since no asset allocation model is immutable, it is not inappropriate to have small deviations between the broad equity and debt categories, although it still makes sense to regularly rebalance among those categories to a specific target range. You may also choose to gradually increase allocations to those underperforming categories as well as to siphon off gains from those overperforming categories. These movements should tend to be nominal (2 to 3 percent would be a considerable shift).

These attempts at catch-up could be viewed as market timing decisions because you are slightly deviating from the model as originally cast. It should also be noted that a recent article in the *Journal of Financial Planning* indicated that performance could be enhanced by chasing returns of the best recent performing funds. I don't find those arguments convincing, though.

In fact, I am more moved by the research by SEI indicating the dispersion of returns from year to year based on manager styles.

Mutual Funds This style-driven allocation is why mutual funds make so much sense for most clients. Mutual funds allow you to tailor the portfolio to the style classes you have defined for your allocation. You can choose specific funds to perform the tasks for which you hire them. Your small cap value fund should be buying small cap value stocks. If they experience a style drift away from why you chose them, you need to justify why you should continue owning them—irrespective of their performance.

This has become more and more complicated. With the acceptance of mutual funds as tools for asset allocation/money management, a $50 million small cap fund could become a $1 billion medium cap fund in a matter of months. Style drift would be thrust upon the manager by cash inflows or outflows.

Unfortunately, information has not completely caught up with the reality of the changing marketplace. It is still difficult to get current information on mutual fund portfolio holdings, making attribution analysis somewhat difficult. This will most likely change in the near future but, until then, attribution analysis on anything other than index funds will be inexact.

There are also arguments regarding how many mutual funds are required in a portfolio. In larger portfolios, if appropriate diversification and efficiency is your client's objective, then he or she would need to own a minimum of 10 funds: cash, corporate or government bonds, international bonds, large US growth and value, small US growth and value, international growth and value, and emerging markets. If you want to have the client own bond funds that have different durations, you would need to increase the number of funds. It may also make sense to include niche funds, such as precious metals or real estate.

The argument that this will diminish overall performance is true only as determined by how you measure performance. If you are trying to outperform an arbitrary benchmark such as the S&P 500, your success in doing so is pure luck. However, if you are attempting to provide your client with reasonable returns and lower risk, this diversified approach is essential. This is why it is critical to frame the discussions with your clients around the choice of risk mitigation (not minimization) rather than total returns.

It is amazing how many times we find ourselves engaged in different arenas with our clients when it comes to absolute performance. The Wealth Management Index establishes the game in which you are operating. The client agrees to the objectives and therefore recognizes the limitations and advantages of asset allocation.

Time Horizon and the CPI   If it is your task to insure that the client meets the objectives as described to you, then it is also your job to be certain those objectives are achievable. Our chances of success are much greater the longer we can keep the client. The market is a series of cycles that has tremendous short-term volatility and relatively modest long-term volatility (and strong relative semivariance because most of the long-term volatility is positive).

Clients want to save money for some future spending. Most clients do not save just for the joy of saving. Since clients are saving for something, the best investment advice will give the clients with reasonable expectations the amount of money that they need when they want it. If that's the case, short-term negative fluctuations in the portfolio are meaningless. As long as the time horizon is long enough to allow for the market cycles to conform (presuming that they will), as mentioned earlier, short-term pullbacks are buying opportunities. In fact, even the pullbacks of 1973 and 1974 only took a little more than 3 years to pay off.

This is not the case with significant positive fluctuations. These are meaningful to the extent that they may allow you to accept less volatility risk. If we have constructed a portfolio that we believe will produce better long-term returns because of our equity exposure and if this portfolio produces considerable returns in a relatively short period of time, then it makes sense to look at the allocation model to see whether it should be changed. Time horizon allows us to do this.

The way to measure whether our clients can meet their spending objectives at the end of the saving rainbow is through tracking the personal CPI of the client. This is the only relevant issue in financial planning. If the stock market went up 10 percent a year, our account was up 11 percent a year, but inflation was at 8 percent a year, we still probably failed. On the other hand, if the market went up 11 percent a year, our account was up 10 percent, and inflation was at 4 percent, we probably succeeded.

Were Your Annual Contributions or Withdrawals at Target?

In the cash flow section of the index we determined the amount of savings and spending that we anticipated taking place. Matching this back into the accumulation section is extremely important. Most of our clients in the accumulation stage of their lives are probably increasing their portfolios anywhere from 3 to 30 percent a year through additional contributions.

Depending on the level of contributions relative to the portfolio, those numbers could be significantly more important than rates of return. Also, these contribution levels impact how the rest of the portfolio should be allocated. For example, a young physician who has accumulated $300,000 and is contributing

$50,000 a year in retirement plans and personal investing would probably have a completely different allocation than would someone who received a $300,000 personal injury settlement and will not be contributing annually. The physician is utilizing de facto dollar cost averaging. Those annual contributions make volatility a godsend.

If the contributions are not made as planned, the portfolio could very quickly become out of alignment. If you designed a higher volatility portfolio because of these expected contributions, you may have made the portfolio more vulnerable than you otherwise would have with a static portfolio.

More important, the lack of those contributions may call into question the validity of the espoused client values. Since all our projection work is based on expectations of spending patterns today *and* tomorrow, the client who is not meeting the saving obligations may not also be realistic about future income needs. This lack of consistency between words and deeds creates the Hobson's choice of dealing with this directly or ultimately failing in your work.

Monitoring withdrawals is arguably even more important. For almost all clients who are withdrawing funds from their portfolios, we establish a spending policy. Through this, a certain percentage of the portfolio is spent (or a certain dollar amount not representing more than a certain percentage of the portfolio) with the hope being that the long-term growth of the portfolio will either exceed the spend down limits or will spend all the assets down concurrent with the culmination of the need for those assets.

For those clients who wish for their portfolios to keep pace with inflation, our upper limit on the spending policy is 6 percent. This does not allow the client to force the portfolio to produce income and therefore enables the client to be more growth oriented. For this structure to be successful, though, the portfolio needs time enough to perform and excessive withdrawals must be curtailed.

In a strong stock market, excess withdrawals do not really matter (unless you are "banking" returns for the times when the market will underperform). In a bad market, excess withdrawals can be disastrous.

Here is a simplified example. If the clients have $1 million with a six percent spending policy, they will be withdrawing $60,000 a year. If they take their withdrawals the first of January, they have $940,000 invested for the year. The account needs to grow by 6.35 percent for the client to be even at the end of the year. On average, this will be attainable.

Averages are deceptive, though. If we earned our 6.35 percent by having a zero return in the first year and a 12.7 percent in the second, utilizing the same $60,000 withdrawal would leave our account worth less than the $1 million with which we started. If we compound that problem by taking excessive withdrawals, our performance may have difficulty catching up to the spending. By having 2 or 3 years of underperformance coupled with excessive withdrawals, we may have dug a hole with our clients from which neither of us can escape.

Clients who spend more than their policy need to be confronted early. A new values assessment must be worked through. If a client is still unable to change this behavior and not live their expressed values, you may need to suspend the relationship or call in outside help. When this happens in our practice, we send our clients to money therapists for counseling.

Was the Portfolio Income Tax-Efficient?

Tax efficiency with portfolios should not be ignored, but it cannot take precedent over returns. When you evaluate the structure of a client's portfolio, you need to do this with an eye toward efficiency. Obviously, you are hoping for the best possible real rate of return consistent with the values and risk tolerance expressed by your client.

There are some very simple steps to enhancing tax efficiency for clients. If you view a couple's portfolio as a combined portfolio and set up an asset allocation appropriate for the total picture, the placement of the investments is important. There are some simple truths about taxation:

1. Capital gains are paid as they are realized.

2. This potential deferral (see (1) above) is a tax break. If there is an additional break between capital gains and ordinary income—wonderful.

3. Qualified money comes out as ordinary income.

4. Losses cannot be deducted in a qualified plan.

5. Tax rates may change over time.

6. To gain the benefit of a stepped-up basis on death, you need to have a gain in the investment.

There are also some simple truths about couples and money:

1. In many cases we segregate investments according to accounts or type. This means that one account will inevitably trail another simply because of the types of investments placed into it. Even though the couple agrees it is joint money, the client whose assets are underperforming is a little resentful. This is especially true if the client with the trailing portfolio is not as sophisticated as his or her partner.

2. People who start off as couples don't necessarily stay couples.

3.   Couples almost always have different money profiles.

This means that tax efficiency may even have to play second fiddle to domestic harmony. Irrespective of this familial disclaimer, it would make the most sense to purchase those
investments that produce the most taxable income in places
where taxable income is irrelevant.

This would make bonds most appropriate in a qualified
account (unless for some reason the tax-free yields are surprisingly close to taxable yields). It would also make sense to own
those stock mutual funds that generate the most ordinary income to be held within the plan. You cannot necessarily judge
this by portfolio turnover. In fact, studies have shown that the
tax differences between funds with portfolio turnover above 15
percent are nominal. This may be because high turnover funds
often sell their losers quickly and let their winners ride.

It would probably make more sense to own those funds with
a higher percentage of their return from dividends in the tax-
efficient plans over those funds with high turnover. Most important, you can look to the history of the portfolio, investigate
built-in gains, and make your decisions accordingly. You will not
be able to manage these portfolios perfectly, though.

Another argument involves the year-end purchase of mutual funds. Here again the mood is mixed. Many people choose
not to buy funds after October since they don't want their clients to get caught with capital gains from investments that they
have only held for 2 months. This must be weighed against the
cost of being out of the market for those 2 months.

It may make more sense to find some funds that don't expect to realize much in capital gains and at least be in the market with the intention of shifting into your desired funds after
distributions have occurred. It may also make sense to realize
losses and replace them with a similar fund for 31 days to avoid

the wash sale rules. If the spread between ordinary income and capital gains is large enough, it may make sense to just invest, realize the gains, and increase your basis in case you want to realize losses in a subsequent year (at ordinary rates).

We did this with emerging market funds during the end of 1995. Many of our clients had losses in their funds. We sold them out of one fund and replaced it with a "similar" emerging market fund. Since no two funds are identical, though, this should be done only when you are very comfortable with the replacement fund.

Have You Set Aside Enough Cash for Purchases to Be Made in the Next Three Years?

Time heals all wounds. If you don't have the time to recover from market cycles then you shouldn't be in the market. This means that if you plan to buy something in the next 2 or 3 years with cash, this cash should stay in cash.

Don't be fooled, though, by time horizons. If your client's 16-year-old is going to college in 2 years, their time horizon is between 2 and 6 years. The longer-term money can be invested in instruments that might have volatility.

This is the same with retirees. You need to invest for their lifetime. Many times people approaching retirement will become more conservative in their retirement plans because they either think that they need the cash when they retire or feel concerned about rolling over their retirement dollars if they have had recent poor performance. The logic is faulty. The allocations should remain consistent even though they may be switching managers. For most retirees, inflation is a greater risk than volatility, although clearly the portfolio must be adjusted somewhat to reflect the fact that contributions have been suspended.

On the other hand, if your client intends to pay cash to purchase a car in the next couple of years, he or she has no business being invested. It is the combination of time and compound interest that provides the magic in investing. Taking away either of those two components makes the risk involved not worth the potential rewards.

This fact is harder and harder to drum home in a good stock market. The Wealth Management Index enables the client to focus on the nature of the need for the money and helps separate the emotion from the reason.

Summary

Investment and accumulation planning represents 25 percent of the index because of its importance. It is one area of the Wealth Management Index, though, where focus is often on the wrong things—rate of returns against benchmarks rather than against objectives, tax avoidance rather than investment performance.

This is also an area where there is much information written, but this information is often disjointed and sometimes off the point. By developing an understanding with your clients as to what you are trying to accomplish, you will assuage their fears and redirect their efforts to what they have told you they wanted.

CASE STUDY

FACTS

Mark and Pat Rogers are 68 and 65, respectively. They are retired and living off their investments and social security. Mark and Pat have five children. When Mark and Pat die, they would like to leave their estate equally to their children. Mark and Pat's parents lived well into their 80s. Mark and Pat are in excellent health.

Mark and Pat own two properties—one in Minneapolis and one in Florida. They live 7 months in Florida and 5 months in Minnesota. The properties have no debt against them.

Their social security pays them $18,000 a year. They have roughly $1 million in retirement plans. They also have $25,000 in a money market fund outside the retirement plan.

They need income of $60,000 from their investments, paid monthly.

The areas on which we needed to focus the Wealth Management Index follow:

1. How did your investments perform against your established target rate of return (CPI plus a stated percentage)?
   - What is the return objective based on the Rogers' personal CPI?
2. Were your annual contributions or withdrawals at target?
   - Are the Rogers withdrawing money according to their spending policy as laid out in the investment policy?
3. Is your asset allocation appropriate?
   - What is the Rogers' investment philosophy?
   - How has the investment policy been established and monitored?
   - Are the Rogers rebalancing as outlined in the policy?
4. How tax-efficient is the Rogers' portfolio?
5. Have you set aside enough cash for anticipated purchases in the next 3 years?

SCORING FOR THE WEALTH MANAGEMENT INDEX

Throughout the year, all these areas were discussed and implemented as described below:

Asset Allocation

Mark and Pat's retirement plan was invested primarily in US Treasuries and utility stocks. This portfolio allocation was set up for income but was not reflective of the Rogers' willingness to accept volatility in the portfolio.

After developing the cash flow projection, we discovered that there would be a low probability of this portfolio keeping pace with their personal inflation rate throughout their life expectancy. They view this inflation risk as greater than the volatility risk associated with trying to grow the portfolio.

We determined that the investment philosophy would be the utilization of a spending policy of 6 percent. We also agreed that our objective was not to maximize absolute returns, but to attempt to provide consistent returns at 6 percent over their personal inflation rate. This personal inflation rate reflects how much their operating costs increase each year on items such as real estate taxes, insurance, groceries, and club memberships.

Through our investment policy, we decided upon a 65 percent stock and 35 percent bond allocation. We also set asset class targets.

We determined expected and acceptable ranges of returns based on their income needs and comfort level. We also set acceptable maximums for both broad asset classes and individual investments. Finally, we established rebalancing parameters.

Pat and Mark worked very hard to help us understand their objectives and lay out an appropriate investment policy. During the year, US stocks outpaced international equities by a significant margin. Pat and Mark did not wish to rebalance to our agreed-upon levels through the sale of US stocks and the purchase of international ones. Even though US stocks actually led international stocks for the entire year, they still score zero points for this piece of the section, but gain all the points for the other areas. Their total score then was 8 points ($100 \times \{(.25 \times .4) \times .8\}$).

Return Against the CPI

The portfolio produced a total return of 14 percent, while their expenses increased 2 percent. This resulted in a return far greater than the needed 8 percent. They scored 2.5 points ($100 \times (.25 \times .1)$).

Contribution/Withdrawals

We determined that the portfolio needed to produce $60,000 for the Rogers. We decided to spend their liquid cash first to give more time for the retirement plan to grow. They received a total of 10 points ($100 \times (.25 \times .4)$).

Tax Efficiency

The Rogers are in the 28 percent marginal federal tax bracket. We deferred some tax by spending their liquid reserves rather than the retirement plan money, but we will still ended up replacing the liquid reserves by the next year. This area for the Rogers does not bear much relevance, although it could once they reach an age where minimum withdrawals from their plans must be made. We still scored all 1.25 points here $(100 \times (.25 \times .05))$.

Cash Needs

The income calculation for the Rogers includes money for car replacement. They have ample liquid reserves and thus scored all 1.25 points $(100 \times (.25 \times .05))$.

SUMMARY

The Rogers earned 23 out of the potential 25 points. It will be important to change the withdrawal rate on the plan for next year, since the assets grew at greater than the anticipated rate.

8

ESTATE PLANNING (DISTRIBUTION)

While inappropriate planning for the disposition of one's estate can be the most costly planning error in terms of overall dollars, it represents only 20 percent of the Wealth Management Index because the building of the estate takes precedence over its distribution. Without careful attention given to the first four areas of the Wealth Management Index, the distribution component's importance will be dramatically reduced. This in no way should minimize the significance of the planning.

This is an area where you find out amazing things about your clients' values. As you discuss goals related to survivorship, you will not only uncover the fears of the surviving spouses, but you will also discover the other spouses' feelings about their own mortality and how they wish to define it. You will almost certainly uncover the clients' true feeling about taxation as you discuss the draconian inheritance tax. You will be able to discern the clients' openness about money as well as the psychological baggage attached to it as you explore what they wish to leave the children. All this information must coalesce with the other areas of the Wealth Management Index.

One of the reasons that this area provides so much information is because of its inevitability and its specter. Death is something that we often tend to ignore, as evidenced in the following quote: "Perhaps the whole root of our trouble is that we will sacrifice all the beauty of our lives, will imprison ourselves in totems, taboos, crosses, blood sacrifices, steeples, mosques, races, armies, flags, nations, in order to deny the fact of death, which is the only fact we have."[1] It is this certainty that makes it so important to plan for, yet so difficult to embrace.

The most important tool in estate planning is the will. The will covers everything from who the clients want to care for their children to who will receive what. The will must be synchronized with the wealth transfer wishes of the client or the tool is not useful. This harmony represents the largest percentage of the index in this category because everything else the client does must presuppose the will is congruent with the client's values.

The second most valued index item involves beneficiary designations. In many ways, this is an extension of the first item. Beneficiary designations must be appropriate or wealth transfer wishes will not be as effective as they need to be. The subtleties, though, of this area make it essential for us to isolate it.

The various permutations of estate planning are obviously important to overall wealth management but are not as meaningful as are the first two areas. Powers of attorney, health care declarations, and living wills help us understand our clients' values regarding everything from incapacity to probate. This is an area of the index that we value relatively low, yet it also is an area in which some planners have based their whole practices. On a relative value scale, these items are important but may not be urgent.

We place as much value on the funding of various trusts as

---

[1] James Baldwin, "Letter from a Region in My Mind," *The New Yorker*, November 1962.

we do on the establishment of them. The "devil is in the details" appropriately describes the funding of trusts. There are countless times where the most ingeniously drawn estate plan is not completed because the client did not follow through on the retitling of assets. If you accept the fact that trusts are not necessarily essential to all estate plans, yet you also recognize that if a trust is appropriate it is only effective if it is funded, then you can see how this funding easily scores as many points as the decision to set up the trust.

Gifts are the last component within this category. Sometimes as planners we become so enamored with the exotic that we lose focus on the ordinary. The simplicity of an appropriate gifting strategy is often more sublime than those aforementioned, sometimes complex, trusts. A gift can be easy, annual, direct, and inexpensive to execute. If the client lives long enough (and is willing to utilize his or her unified credit), he or she can often gift millions of dollars on a gift and estate tax-free basis. Walt Whitman said in *Leaves of Grass,* "The art of art, the glory of expression and the sunshine of the light of letters, is simplicity."[2]

Percent of Index (20%) for Estate Planning (Distribution)

	Percent of Distribution Scale	Total Index Weight
Does your will match your wealth transfer wishes?	40%	8%
Are your assets titled correctly and have you set up appropriate beneficiary designations?	25	5
Have you established and funded all the necessary trusts?	15	3
Do you need and have • Power of attorney? • Health care declaration? • Living will?	15	3
Have you made your desired gifts for this year?	5	1

[2] Walt Whitman, *Leaves of Grass* (New York: Penguin Classics, 1959), p. 12.

Does Your Will Match Your Wealth Transfer Wishes?

There is the story of the tightwad who was on his deathbed and called to his side his three most trusted advisors—his doctor, his minister, and his lawyer. He told them that his wish was to be buried with a significant amount of his money and instructed each of them to cast $500,000 next to him in the open coffin at the viewing. The miser soon died.

The trusted advisors gathered after the burial and the guilt became too much for the doctor. He said, "I had to put up with that irascible old man throughout his illness and yet I deal with many indigent patients in need of my services. I did not completely comply with his wishes. I did throw $400,000 into the coffin, but I kept $100,000 for myself so that I may help those without the resources to pay me."

The minister breathed a slight sigh of relief and said, "I have dedicated countless hours enhancing this man's spiritual journey. While he didn't explicitly say so, I know that he recognized our parish needed repairs. I therefore did not completely comply with his stated request. I placed in the casket $300,000 but set aside $200,000 to meet his unstated objectives."

The lawyer sneered at the two other advisors. "As the person responsible for the financial health of this man, I saw what you did and how you tried to justify it. Although he was a miser, he paid me significant fees throughout his life. I therefore decided that his dying wishes should be granted and I made the decision to accommodate him and make up for your malfeasance. I pulled the cash out of the coffin and threw in a check to cover the whole amount."

Needless to say, truly understanding and ferreting out the client's wealth transfer wishes is a difficult task. While a good estate planning attorney should be part of any financial team, we still play a huge role in assuring our client that this area is adequately studied. Setting objectives is the first step.

There are a myriad of objectives related to wealth transfer. We must cut through all the emotional flak to get to the core desires of the client and resolve the transfer problems. The core issue is: *In a perfect world, to whom do you want and don't you want your money to go when you die?* If you can start with this understanding, then you can tackle the emotional items one by one.

For instance, what if parents express a concern about how their children would spend a large inheritance? The easiest solution is to set up trusts with spendthrift provisions, varying distribution dates, limited Crummey powers, and with a trustee who views the money as his or her own.

While this might provide an answer, it may not really address the issues. The parents want the children to have their money. That is their primary desire. They have several secondary and tertiary wishes as well. They may want to be able to control the children from their grave. They would like to impose their values around money on their children. They may also wish for the children to appreciate this legacy in spite of its several strings. They may be quite surprised if the children view this as a yoke around their necks that can ultimately lead to the very behavior the parents are most concerned with controlling.

If we know to whom the money should go, we can then address these emotional issues in a number of ways. We can forge ahead with a plan that labels the children and asks for none of their input. We could have family meetings with the parents and their children in which we discuss some of the money issues. We may even encourage money counseling.

There is no way that we can get to the root of the parents' apprehensions and motivations, though, without really understanding to whom they want the money to go.

It is also important to understand to whom the money should not go. The government is one inheritor that many people wish to expunge. The surviving spouse's potential new partner is another. Once again, though, it is important to filter the whys around this only after you have identified the whos.

The whos can sometimes appear to be at cross purposes with the whys. The client may wish for his or her spouse to get the money, but not the spouse's new husband or wife. Unfortunately, our clients can sometimes solve for the question that was not asked and therefore constrain themselves from having all their wishes met. The best way to muddle through this is through continuing to ask, "In a perfect world, to whom do you want and don't you want your money to go when you die?"

Once clients have settled on who should and should not get their money, the real fun starts. The greatest thing about estate planning is you get to realize your clients' dreams with them. An estate plan is the chance to look with your clients down from the clouds at their life. It is a time to again dream with clients and to actually experience the realization of those dreams.

One exercise to try to understand the clients' motivations is to get them to write their own obituary. As long as you are on the subject of death, this process (as morbid as it may seem) will help you affirm the other work that you are doing. This look back over a lifetime will help you see more clearly what clients want from their lives.

Once you have established with your clients their objectives around wealth transfer, you can then send them to a qualified estate planning attorney to help them realize those objectives through a properly drafted will. The will should be set up, for example, prior to the retitling of assets because this is the framework for the decisions. The will establishes things such as the credit trust to maximize the unified credit of both spouses. It is also through this process that clients can make decisions regarding what other strategies may be appropriate to employ.

All our clients have wills, they just may not know who drafted them. If the client did not choose to draft a will personally or through an attorney, the state in which he or she resides drafted it for them. This is intestacy. A court gets to appoint the guardian for that client's children and to decide who gets to manage the assets for those children. In this era of devolution, this is not an attractive option for most clients.

It is also important to note here that if both spouses are not US citizens, a will is critical even if they don't fear intestacy. The 1988 Tax Act has eliminated the unlimited marital deduction if the decedent's surviving spouse is not a US citizen. Gay and lesbian partners also face this obstacle.

Since the will is the basic document for asset transference, it must be set up in accordance with the client's wealth transfer wishes to score the maximum available points here. While many asset transference ideas can be done outside the will, this is still the document decisions will revert to if timely execution with the other strategies has not been successfully completed.

Are Your Assets Titled Correctly and Have You Set Up Appropriate Beneficiary Designations?

Once the will has been established, you need to look at the assets that the clients have and be sure that they are titled appropriately. You also need to be certain that those assets that may pass outside the will (life insurance, retirement plans, transfer on death brokerage accounts) have correct beneficiaries.

Beneficiary designations provide tremendous planning opportunities and need to be explored in far greater detail. Even the most simple instrument—the IRA—has incredible potential for the client who has amassed significant dollars in it. An IRA can be taxed three times—estate tax, income tax, and an excise tax. *Due to various phaseouts, in a worst case scenario, the total taxes paid on the margins for a tax deferred vehicle can be 108.5 percent!* For the philanthropic client, naming a charity as the beneficiary on the IRA avoids estate and income taxes, but not excise tax. The client can even split IRAs to set the amount of the gift.

The splitting of IRAs can also make sense for the client who has enough money in other places so his or her spouse does not need to receive all the IRA proceeds. By splitting the IRA and naming children as beneficiaries, the client is often able to take out less money under the required minimum distribution rules and the children have a valuable asset that can grow for them for years (if the children choose to make the IRA a decedent IRA).

If the client has reached the required minimum distribution age and has named a non-spouse (typically a child) as the beneficiary of the IRA, he or she must take the minimum distributions using the special 10-year differential rule (minimum distribution incidental benefit requirement or MDIB). This means that the age differential for withdrawals is deemed to be not greater than 10 years.

Once the client passes away after selecting the term-certain distribution method, the beneficiary then may recalculate life expectancy using a joint-life table that accurately represents the age difference. It is important that term-certain was used; recalculation may only be used by the original owner. If withdrawals occurred using the MDIB rules, then term-certain was invariably utilized.

If the child beneficiary is a minor, it may be appropriate to name a custodian under an UTMA rather than to have the courts potentially appoint a guardian.

Another beneficiary alternative would be to set up split-interest trusts where income would go to the heirs and the remainder would go to a charity. Since charitable remainder annuity and unitrusts are exempt from income tax, the trust receives the proceeds tax free.

Surprisingly, it may even make sense (if there is no surviving spouse) for the grantor to withdraw all the proceeds from the tax deferred account prior to death so that he or she can pay the income tax on the asset, thereby reducing the amount of the estate and the accompanying estate tax.

Unlike many other areas of the Wealth Management Index, once choices are made with regard to beneficiaries and the client has died, the cornucopia of opportunities have pretty much dried up. There is not much left but to second guess the decisions. It makes those decisions somewhat frightening. Tweedledum said in *Through the Looking Glass*, "I'm very brave generally, only today I happen to have a headache."[3] Tweedledum could easily have been a financial planner working with a client on a complex estate. I encourage you to buy J. K. Lasser's *How to Pay Less Taxes on Your Retirement Savings* as a reference tool.[4]

Titling of assets can often be used as another will-substitute technique. We are all familiar with the various ways to title assets. Most married couples tend to hold assets individually or as joint tenants with rights of survivorship. Assets that are held jointly with right of survivorship pass outside the will. This typically does involve a sharing of control of the asset which may make the client uncomfortable.

The problem with titling, though, is that if not done correctly, the default position may not be desirable. For example, if an elderly parent wants to place a child's name on a brokerage account and the account is not labeled as joint tenants with right of survivorship, most states will treat the ownership as tenants in common. As tenants in common, each owner owns a proportionate share of the asset. This does not avoid probate on the share owned by the deceased.

Another form of joint ownership that is available in many states is tenancy by the entirety. This type of ownership provides

---

[3] Lewis Carroll, *Through the Looking Glass* (New York: Bantam Classics, 1981), p. 151.

[4] Seymour Goldberg, J. K. Lasser's *How to Pay Less Tax on Your Retirement Savings* (New York: Macmillan General Reference, 1995).

some living creditor protection that is not an attribute of the other joint tenancies.

There is a lesser known titling opportunity currently available in several states. The Uniform Transfer on Death Security Registration Act allows clients to title assets so that they are not considered to be jointly held, yet the assets are still able to pass directly to the named survivor. These transfer on death accounts can be set up with mutual fund shares or securities held in street name at brokerage firms. Interestingly, even if the state in which your client lives has not approved of this procedure, if the state of the issuer of the security, or the transfer agent's state, has adopted this, the act may still be an option.

Clearly the area around beneficiary and titling decisions can be a huge determinant in the success of the overall wealth management for the client. This is an area that needs to be gone through and affirmed in order to capture all the available points in the index. As you go through the titling of the client's assets, it is also a good time to establish an inventory of what the client owns and where everything is kept. This inventory should be in a safe place at home, with another copy kept away from the home but not in a safe deposit box. It should be kept away from home so that it is not harmed in case of fire or theft. It should not be kept in a safe deposit box because access to the inventory is critical and this access could be limited at time of death. You may choose to keep a copy on a floppy disk and a hard copy in the client file. Not only does this inventory help for property/ casualty purposes, it is also helpful for the surviving spouse (especially if he or she has little financial acumen) and heirs.

Have You Established and Funded All the Necessary Trusts? Have You Made Your Desired Gifts for this Year?

If the estate justifies it, planning techniques using various gifts and trusts can be employed. There is a tendency to over plan in these areas, though. The object of this piece of the Wealth Management Index is to satisfy the client's objectives as to wealth transference. One of the often unstated, but usually important, objectives to the client is simplicity. The planner must constantly evaluate the marginal benefits of the strategies employed so that the client does not become frustrated with the complexity of the plan and ultimately not follow it.

Planning can be done through gifts and trusts while the client is living and/or upon death through a will. In large estates, it often makes sense to evaluate making annual gifts. One of the things we need to be careful about in recommending such a strategy is to not encourage our clients to gift so many assets that his or her own quality of life is obstructed. A strong stock market can lull us with our estimates of portfolio growth, thereby causing us to suggest gifts greater than what might prove to be reasonable.

A large estate is really a relative term. Many clients feel that if they have $1 million invested, they have a large estate. While this is true relative to the rest of the population, utilizing a 6 percent spending policy, this would only create $60,000 a year in income to spend. This amount may be considerably less than what the client who amassed those dollars needs.

We need to be sure that the clients can understand how their dollars work for them and that the ultimate objective in accumulating assets for retirement is the conversion of predominately growth into predominately spending power. The grail is not $1 million in the bank but rather the ability to maintain the lifestyle they desire. Only after cash flow can be assured should we begin to contemplate gifts.

If the purpose of the gift is to shrink the estate, then there could be a variety of assets that are most suitable to give. Cash is often the easiest asset because its basis is its value. It may make sense to gift assets that have little current gain but would be expected to grow a great deal (private stock, raw land). It usually does not make sense to gift low-basis investments because the client foregoes the step-up in basis at death. It almost never makes sense to gift assets in which there is a loss.

It may also be appropriate to make lifetime gifts that begin to utilize the unified credit, although this type of decision needs to be carefully reviewed. There are various ways to leverage this credit so using it for the simple gift may not be the best use of this valuable tool.

A personal residence trust (PRT) or a qualified personal residence trust (QPRT) can be methods to shift large dollars out of the estate. A house grantor-retained income trust (GRIT) also allows the client to stay in the family house for a particular term. This means that the client is really making a gift of the future interest in the residence—a gift for unified credit purposes that would actually be discounted. The clients must outlive the terms of the GRIT in order for them to remove the residence from their estate.

If the client does not want to give up a residence, he or she can set up a GRAT (grantor retained annuity trust) or GRUT (grantor retained unitrust). The client would receive the income from the trust. This is a leveraging technique only to the extent that the growth of the underlying asset exceeds the income from the asset. The value of the gift is determined based on 120 percent of the federal midterm rate at the time the GRAT is established.

As previously discussed, life insurance trusts can also be set up to attempt to leverage the available unified credit.

For the very wealthy, each parent also has a $1 million generation-skipping transfer available to them. This can be a tremendous benefit, especially if property that is expected to appreciate is used to fund a dynasty trust. The rules around these trusts are quite complex and require the work of a very competent estate planning attorney. If a dynasty trust is a testamentary trust (to be funded upon the death of the grantor), the client needs to be sure that it is set up appropriately to get the maximum funding.

If there is a qualified terminable interest property (QTIP) trust set up for the clients after a first death, it may be difficult to insure that the full $1 million will go to the grandchildren. Typically, a credit trust is set up with a QTIP. In this case, only the dollars from the credit trust will qualify for the generation-skipping tax exemption on the first death. This can be amplified, though, if a reverse QTIP election is allowed. Essentially, a separate GST QTIP trust will be set up under the will of the first spouse to die.

There are some very important components to be included in a dynasty trust, which are too detailed to discuss for our purposes. This tool, though, is incredibly effective and essentially can allow $2 million, plus the appreciation on these assets if set up as a lifetime transfer, to be passed without the 55 percent generation-skipping tax. Don't be confused, though. These trusts are still subjected to gift limitations and therefore can use up the unified credit.

Life insurance is one asset that can be bought in a dynasty trust. If the client utilizes his or her unified credit to fund life insurance trusts and if this is combined with a dynasty trust, then literally millions of dollars could pass to the grandchildren free from the generation-skipping transfer tax.

If the clients are not US citizens, then you should explore a qualified domestic trust. These, too, are quite complex and provide only limited relief, but they should not be ignored.

Although not a trust, the family limited partnership is another strategy to reduce the size of the estate. The reason that this can be effective is that the assets placed in the partnership are often valued higher than the units of the partnership gifted to the kids. This is because of minority discounts and lack of marketability discounts.

Family limited partnerships provide a number of advantages. They enable the parents to make much larger gifts without using their unified credit. The parents are also often able to retain control of the vehicles placed in the partnership because the parents serve as the general partners. This is a huge advantage over trusts where there can be a risk that this control will bring the asset back into the parents' estate.

Living Trusts   Living trusts have been touted as the estate planning panacea. I do not believe that these are for everyone. There are several benefits of a living trust:

1. It can help you avoid probate. Probate in the minds of many clients is worse than Dante's 9th Circle of Hell. In most cases, this is overblown. Probate exists to help estates transfer property when the owner dies. Probate validates the will. Probate also extinguishes claims against the estate. Depending on the state in which the client lives, assets do not have to be tied up during the probate process. Probate can be expensive at times, especially if costs are fixed as a percentage of the estate. Some states, like Minnesota, have simplified probate procedures which make it relatively painless.

2. By avoiding probate, lists of your property don't become part of the public record.

3. Assets transfer relatively easily because they stay in the trust. If the client was the trustee for his or her own living trust, then only the trustee changes upon death.

The problem with these living trusts is that it costs money to set them up and to transfer the property into them. They can also be a pain to continue to effect transactions in throughout the client's lifetime. These are not the client's assets anymore, they are the trust's. While this appears to be transparent, for certain transactions it is not. Also, unless all the client's assets are registered in the trust, they will have to go through probate anyway. This can frustrate the heirs to no end.

Living trusts can make sense, especially in high-expense probate states. It can also make sense to place property that a client owns outside of his or her state of residence into a living trust. This will avoid the need for ancillary probate. They are also a tool for the client who is worried about incapacity. The client would not need to fund the trust immediately, but could gradually move money into the trust. Someone else could be named to manage the assets and there could also be provisions set up to have the client removed as trustee should he or she be declared incompetent to manage the trust.

Charity Planning One of the easiest ways to avoid estate tax is to have the client give away assets to charity. These gifts remove the asset from the estate. Unfortunately, they can also remove any of the asset's income potential from the heirs as well.

The Bible says, "Charity shall cover the multitude of sins."[5] Oscar Wilde said, "Charity creates a multitude of sins."[6] It doesn't much matter which view the client has, it is still essential to explore philanthropy in the Wealth Management Index. Charitable intent may not be as obvious as one may think. For example, someone who indicates a desire to make a difference in the world may not necessarily feel compelled to do it through gifts of capital. On the other hand, I have had clients who gave nothing to charity throughout their lifetime, but desired to make substantial gifts upon their death.

---

[5] *The Bible*, I Peter 4:8.

[6] Oscar Wilde, *The Soul of Man Under Socialism* in *The Columbia Dictionary of Quotations*, ed. Robert Andrews (New York: Columbia University Press, 1993), p. 133.

As mentioned earlier, it may make sense to name a charity as the beneficiary of retirement plans, thereby bypassing estate and income tax consequences with an asset that is more expensive to sell because of taxes than cash or securities. We also discussed the value of gifting appreciated stock to a charity during one's lifetime to circumvent the capital gains costs.

In situations in which there is an intense philanthropical desire, there are other devices that should be explored. A charitable lead trust can be set up. In this case, the charity gets the income interest and the remaining interest goes to the family. The income ratio that is set up, as well as the time horizon on the gift, will determine the amount of the charitable deduction for income or estate tax purposes. The leverage of this concept for estate planning is that the trust could grow at a rate greater than the income paid to the charity. If this happens, the heirs reap the benefit of this enhanced performance.

A charitable remainder trust is the exact opposite. The income beneficiaries of the trust are the clients or their children. The charity gets the asset after the death of the income beneficiaries or after the term of the trust. The gift is an irrevocable commitment and permanently removes the asset from the estate.

Many planners use charity in estate planning as a tool with which to leverage the estate. They show printouts that depict how by giving to charity, typically in the form of a net income make up charitable remainder unitrust (NIMCRUT), clients will actually have more money than if they were to die with the asset in their estate. The incidents of this being true are relatively inconsequential when compared with the incidents of the charity coming out ahead of the clients. This is why we always tell our clients to use these types of devices only if they are charitably inclined.

Assets that are gifted to charities may be different from those assets which you recommend gifting to your client's children. For example, it often makes sense to gift assets that are appreciating rapidly to the children so that they may reap the growth while removing this ever-increasing estate tax propagator from the estate. On the other hand, it is in the client's best interest to gift this kind of asset to a charity after it has realized its value so as to receive the maximum income tax deduction possible.

My own situation shows that this rule of thumb is not always true. Bridget (my wife) and I gifted a mutual fund that had appreciated in value (and had a change in management style so we wanted to dispose of it) to a gift trust set up by a large mutual fund company. We were therefore able to deduct the full value of the gift at the time it was made. We gave more in value than what our charitable inclinations were because we wanted to get rid of the fund that we had held for a long time and in which we had sizable unrealized gains. We also wanted to have the money continue to grow in this gift trust.

We are now able to continue to meet many of our charitable commitments without continuing to fund the trust. While we don't get to deduct the appreciation on the gift once it is in the trust, we also don't have to use our cash flow to fund all our charitable needs. We can invest our saved cash flow into a new mutual fund that we feel has a better chance of outperforming the fund we gifted.

Trust planning offers tremendous opportunities for wealth building. I recommend *The Book of Trusts* published by Leimberg Associates Books as an excellent reference tool for this work.[7]

---

[7] Charles K. Plotnik, Stephan R. Leimberg, and Russell E. Miller, *The Book of Trusts* (Bryn Mawr, PA: Leimberg Associates, 1996).

Do You Need and Have a Power of Attorney, a Health Care Declaration, and a Living Will?

While this area constitutes only 3 percent of the Wealth Management Index, it may be the single most emotionally charged area in the entire index. Most of the previous discussion centered on what to do with asset disposition. This area deals primarily with the personal. How do your clients want their wishes to be carried out should they no longer be in a position to do so themselves? Lest you think this is not a big deal, consider the last time you asked your spouse to perform a simple task that you normally do. Did you feel any need to correct him or her?

The power of attorney can be a broad document appointing the attorney-in-fact to anything that would legally be allowed to be delegated. It can also be quite narrow in its scope, limiting the attorney-in-fact to one particular act. This must be executed when the client has the capacity to act, but one of the nice things about it is that it does not require a "judicial definition of disability to go into effect."[8]

It almost always makes sense to establish a durable power of attorney which continues upon the incapacity of the principal. These terminate upon the death of the principal. It also is usually appropriate to execute a general power of attorney which creates a much broader scope of authority. There are obviously legitimate psychological hurdles to jump over before this tool should be used. If set up with springing powers, it would only go into effect upon the incapacity of the principal. This may be more palatable to the control-oriented client.

More important, to effectively use a vehicle like this, the clients should have thoroughly discussed their wishes and values around their property rights. The time spent on the front

---

[8] *Tax Management Inc.* (Washington, DC: BNA, Inc., 1990), section 475:1006.

end will potentially eliminate the risk of not having their wishes carried out. For wealth management purposes, it is the discussion that we are measuring not the decision.

The other key area involved in incapacity planning is the durable power of attorney for health care. This gives the attorney-in-fact the power to make health care decisions when, in the judgment of the attending physician, the principal is unable to make or communicate that decision. This is the core document for the decision to withhold support through artificial means.

This area needs to be understood by the clients. I just had a situation where a client's mother, who heretofore had been in excellent health, suffered a stroke and was in a coma. The doctors said that she had no chance of a full recovery. If she did recover she would be severely brain damaged. My client had not discussed this area in detail with her mother, yet had the power of the appointment. While the responsibility for the decision fell squarely on her shoulders, she did not have the background to make a choice. The mother passed away before she had to.

Our responsibility is to graphically lay out the dilemma our clients face should this area not be discussed. While you may feel that you have no desire at all to be under life support, are you completely comfortable making that decision for your spouse or parent without a discussion around it? Our index forces us to explore the subject to score the points.

Summary

The distribution aspect of the wealth management index needs to be completely integrated with all the other areas of the index to be effective. We also need to do our best to help our clients implement those changes to have their plans match their desires. This is probably the area of the wealth management index where it is easiest to leave some loose ends. Unfortunately, it is also the most expensive place for this to happen.

CASE STUDY

FACTS

Edie Dolan is a 68-year-old widow with three grown children and two grandchildren. She has an estate of approximately $1.5 million, of which $700,000 are invested in a retirement plan, $300,000 are invested in a home, $400,000 are held in cash and marketable securities, and $100,000 are in personal property. She has no debt. She also has no life insurance.

Edie's income is satisfied through her social security and pension plan. She is not living off any of her investments. She has an excellent relationship with her children, each of whom asked her to live with them when she became widowed.

Edie wishes to pass her estate equally to her children. Since she is not spending her assets, she would just as soon have her children have access to the money. Edie is not insurable.

In establishing the Wealth Management Index, we looked at the following areas:

1. Does your will match your wealth transfer wishes?
   - Has Edie fully discussed the areas of her estate plan?
   - Have the necessary documents been drafted?
2. Do you need and have a power of attorney, a health care declaration, and a living will?
   - Has a frank and complete discussion taken place regarding incapacity planning and final wishes?
   - Are written procedures established?
3. Are your assets titled correctly and are your beneficiary designations appropriate?
   - Do all assets entitled to a beneficiary designation have one?
   - Is the retirement established consistently with Edie's objectives?
   - Do the correct people own the right assets?

4. Have you established and funded all the necessary trusts?

+ Has Edie decided what trusts may be appropriate for her?
+ Have they actually been established and funded?

SCORING FOR THE WEALTH MANAGEMENT INDEX

Will

Edie was very clear with her estate planning wishes. She wanted to pass on as much as possible to her children, was more concerned with estate taxes than control, and felt that her children would take care of her should something happen.

Since Edie was not spending her investments currently and would be compelled to begin withdrawing from her retirement plan relatively shortly, it was apparent that her estate was going to continue to grow at a fairly rapid pace. It was also obvious that estate taxes could be a major issue.

Edie's will was set up to provide that her estate be divided evenly among the children. She also wished to give her local hospital somewhere around $100,000 in the name of her late husband. This was detailed in the will. We modified the charitable request by splitting off some of her retirement plan and naming the charity as beneficiary. By setting up a separate retirement plan for $70,000, Edie felt that the gift would grow to be an adequate level when she died. This also took an asset that the children may have some difficulty accessing, instead of giving liquid money to the charity.

Edie felt that her children were old enough and responsible enough to handle her money when she dies, so she was not interested in the establishment of trusts to control the portfolio after her death.

The will was basically quite simple, predominately providing for the equal splitting of the estate. When coupled with other planning techniques, this served Edie's primary objective of splitting the estate.

Edie scored 8 points ($100 \times (.4 \times .2)$).

Power of Attorney, Health Care Declaration, and Living Will

We set up a family meeting to thoroughly discuss Edie's wishes. The meeting included all of Edie's children and the estate planning lawyer. It was decided that for incapacity planning, it made sense to establish a springing power of attorney. We also set up a health care declaration because Edie was not interested in continuing to live via life support. We also decided upon the type of funeral Edie would like to have, including who would be speaking and her desired music!

Edie earned 3 points here ($100 \times (.28 \times .15)$).

Asset Titling/Gifting

The asset titling and beneficiary area was one where there was a tremendous amount of planning necessary. This area also had to be synchronized with a gifting program. Edie was not spending down her assets. She had an estate tax problem that was going to be ever-increasing. She was young enough so that she could eventually gift her way out of this issue. This was because she had no control issues with her children.

Edie's IRA was worth $700,000 and was growing. Even after splitting out a portion for the charity, it was still a large asset that was going to continue to increase. We decided to set up three new retirement plans with each child as the beneficiary, and each child's family as the secondary beneficiary.

We had $400,000 of marketable securities and cash, none of which had much in capital gains. We decided to gift $350,000 of this to the children, thereby using some of the unified credit. Edie did not need these dollars and felt that it would be better if they grew in the children's name rather than hers.

We also began to withdraw money from the IRAs, even though Edie did not need the cash. We withdrew at a rate that would keep her in the 28 percent tax bracket, and then annually gifted those dollars to the children. It was determined that if Edie began to withdraw the money and paid the tax, the resultant transfer would be greater than if both income taxes and estate taxes were paid on the inheritance. The gifts would be equal for each child. No gifts would be made to the grandchildren because of equalization concerns.

Edie scored 6 points ($100 \times (.2 \times .25) + 100 \times (.2 \times .05)$).

Trusts

After careful review, it was decided not to set up living trusts. We also rejected the establishment of a personal residence trust. There was a high probability that Edie would be moving into a smaller home or potentially would move in with one of her children in the next 3 years. We gave Edie 3 points $(100 \times (.2 \times .15))$.

SUMMARY

Edie received all 20 points in this section. Her ongoing planning clearly must integrate this component of the Wealth Management Index with the others to ensure that effective tax decisions have been executed and that the income and control needs do not change.

9

SUMMARY

"Nothing astonishes men so much as common sense and plain dealing."

Ralph Waldo Emerson
Essays, First Series: Art

The Wealth Management Index is many things. It is a client expectation management tool. It can be a performance appraisal device. It can be the radar to help the client find his or her way to financial success. But in my mind, the most important thing that the Wealth Management Index represents is sensibility. If used properly, your clients can rest assured that you have together looked at their situation, developed appropriate goals and strategies, and regularly review the progress toward their objectives.

By laying out the areas of financial planning through the Wealth Management Index, you have taken a seemingly overwhelming role and reduced it to a measurement that the client can relate to and own. This does not minimize your contribution but rather defines it. The regular review in all the areas of the Wealth Management Index provides ongoing affirmation of the value of planning toward goals. Thoreau said, "In the long run, men only hit what they aim at." The Wealth Management Index ensures that the client's target is always clearly viewed through his or her scope.

This book could have been a tome on financial planning. Instead, I hope that it brought up useful ideas to make you more effective and has inspired you to delve deeper into the fine, more detailed works available within each area of the index.

As you work with your satisfied clients over the years, keep score of the successes you have had together, keep track of the annual results of the Wealth Management Index, and do the work that makes this such a meaningful profession.

APPENDIXES

Engagement Letter

March 15, 1996
Ross and Bridget Levin
1111 Avenue S
Minneapolis, MN 55409

Dear Ross and Bridget,

Thank you for coming in the other day and reviewing your situation.

I would like to outline for you my understanding of your situation and discuss the goals as outlined to me in our conversations.

You have managed to build up significant assets. Ross is employed at Mercy where he currently earns $190,000 of salary and a $73,000 bonus. He also earns an additional $80,000–$120,000 from his private practice work. Bridget serves as Ross's business manager.

You have two children. One is at Valparaiso University in Indiana and the other is in eleventh grade.

You have very little debt. You have a mortgage on the first property for $280,000.

It is your objective to retire in five years, sell your house in Minneapolis, and move to Arizona. You would also like to sell the building in which you are currently working.

Page 2

You currently are saving all the interest payments from your property. You also anticipate a contract for deed to be maturing shortly.

We would be working with you on a total wealth management approach. In working together, we would spend significant time on five key areas, making sure that these resonate with your goals and objectives.

1. Asset Protection

We will be covering three areas within this category. We need to be certain that your business interests are adequately covered and would spend time working with you and Jim (your business manager) to be sure that is the case with the Mercy practice. We would also see if there is any way that we can develop a procedure to garner some dollars out of the private practice should you actually retire in five years.

We will also spend time reviewing your life insurance. It appears that you own a significant amount of life insurance with large cash values. We will need to evaluate whether this insurance is appropriate given the other significant assets that you currently have.

Last, we will work with you to see how you are protected from catastrophic loss due to property, casualty, or liability issues. This is especially pronounced due to the real estate operations.

Page 3

2. Disability and Income Protection

In this area, we will work with you to be sure that you are adequately covered from a disability standpoint. We will also spend some time going through what kind of cash flow you expect to have this year and how it will be distributed. You are in a situation where you are saving a lot of your income; we need to determine whether this is being saved in the most appropriate fashion.

We will also spend time reviewing your taxes to be sure that you are paying no more than what you need to be and to see if there are any other areas of planning that we can incorporate here.

3. Debt Management

You indicated that your only debt was a 5.5% mortgage for $290,000, although on the personal financial statement I also see a loan listed through FHA for $90,000. Please clarify that.

This area is one in which we will not need to spend much time because you have done a nice job of controlling your debt and the current borrowing level you are at is very conservative given the rest of your assets.

Page 4

4. Investment Planning

We will work to develop an appropriate investment policy and therefore set up an effective asset allocation policy. We need to have congruity between your investments and your somewhat aggressive retirement objectives.

We will also work with you to make sure the portfolio is tax-efficient.

5. Estate Planning

We need to make sure that your will matches your wealth transfer wishes. We also want to explore powers of attorney, health care declarations, and living wills.

We need to make decisions regarding any gifting strategies as well as ensure that we have set up appropriate trusts.

Last, we need to be certain that the beneficiary designations on your accounts are consistent with your wealth transfer wishes. We also need to explore whether splitting retirement accounts makes sense given your early retirement objectives.

Ross and Bridget, your situation is interesting and complex. I feel that we can do an effective job of working with

Page 5

you to satisfy your goals. Our fee for working together would be $5,000 for the first year plus 1% of any assets that we subsequently manage. In future years, we will charge 1% of the assets that we manage, with a minimum fee of $3,000.

Please call me with any questions you may have. Should you wish to proceed, please endorse the enclosed agreements and mail them back to me with your check made payable to Accredited Investors, Inc., for $2,500.

I look forward to talking with you.

Best regards,

Ross Levin, CFP
President

RL/amg

Wealth Management Index (WMI)

Asset Protection ("Preservation") Index Weight = 25%

% of Asset Protection Scale	Total Index Weight	Category	% of Category	% of Asset Protection Scale	Performance Score (1–10)	Total Index Weight	"WMI" Score
33%	8.25%	Do you have an appropriate amount of life insurance, consistent with an articulated philosophy?					
		1. Develop a philosophy.	45%	14.85%	8	3.71%	2.97
		2. Implement the philosophy.	45%	14.85%	9	3.71%	3.34
		3. Do estate tax analysis.	10%	3.30%	10	0.83%	0.83
33%	8.25%	Have you protected yourself against catastrophic loss due to long-term care, property losses, liability issues?					
		1. Dictate parameters around property/casualty insurance purchase.	50%	16.50%	10	4.13%	4.13
		2. Make decisions regarding long-term care.	25%	8.25%	7	2.06%	1.44
		3. Decide whether asset transference or retitling is appropriate for liability or long-term care concerns.	25%	8.25%	6	2.06%	1.24
34%	8.50%	Are your business interests adequately covered?					
		1. Verify appropriate business form.	34%	11.56%	10	2.89%	2.89
		2. Perform valuation.	16%	5.44%	9	1.36%	1.22
		3. Establish keep/sell agreements.	25%	8.50%	8	2.13%	1.70
		4. Determine funding for death and disability.	25%	8.50%	7	2.13%	1.49
100.00%	25.00%	**Total**		100.00%			21.24

Disability and Income Protection ("Protection " Index Weight = 20%)

% of Disability and Income Scale	Total Index Weight	Category	% of Category	% of Disability and Income Scale	Performance Score (1-10)	Total Index Weight	"WMI" Score
40%	8.00%	Do you have too much or too little disability protection given assets/income & will it pay you if unable to work?					
		1. Assess the income needs if disabled.	45%	18.00%	8	3.60%	2.88
		2. Discuss the value of self-funding.	10%	4.00%	9	0.80%	0.72
		3. Implement or self-insure.	45%	18.00%	10	3.60%	3.60
20%	4.00%	Did you receive income from all sources (earnings, gifts social security, pensions) that was expected this year?					
		1. Discuss expected income & timing this year.	60%	12.00%	10	2.40%	2.40
		2. Estab. items for which client may exert timing discretion.	30%	6.00%	7	1.20%	0.84
		3. Ensure client applies for all benefits entitled to.	10%	2.00%	6	0.40%	0.24
20%	4.00%	Did you spend according to plan?					
		1. Develop the cash flow plan.	50%	10.00%	10	2.00%	2.00
		2. Manage back to the model.	50%	10.00%	9	2.00%	1.80
20%	4.00%	Did you use all reasonable means to reduce your taxes?					
		1. Prepare a tax estimate and determine marginal federal tax bracket + benefit of straddle between years.	30%	6.00%	10	1.20%	1.20
		2. Review/implement all approp. tax reduction strategies.	30%	6.00%	10	1.20%	1.20
		3. Provide stock option planning.	20%	4.00%	7	0.80%	0.56
		4. Evaluate charitable planning, asset transference, and investment tax minimization.	20%	4.00%	6	0.80%	0.48
100.00%	20.00%	**Total**		100.00%			17.92

Debt Management ("Leverage") Index Weight = 10%

% of Debt Management Scale	Total Index Weight	Category	% of Category	% of Debt Management Scale	Performance Score (1–10)	Total Index Weight	"WMI" Score
30%	3.00%	Have you access to as much debt as reasonably possible and at the best available rates?					
		1. Obtain the most free credit available for the client.	70%	21.00%	10	2.10%	2.10
		2. Negotiate the rates and guarantees/covenants.	30%	9.00%	9	0.90%	0.81
40%	4.00%	Is your current ratio better than 2:1 and is your total debt reasonable as a percentage of assets?					
		1. Determine whether current ratio is better than 2:1.	50%	20.00%	10	2.00%	2.00
		2. Review overall debt use relative to assets and income.	50%	20.00%	7	2.00%	1.40
20%	2.00%	Have you managed your debt as expected?	100%	20.00%	10	2.00%	2.00
10%	1.00%	Is your debt tax-efficient?	100%	10.00%	10	1.00%	1.00
100.00%	10.00%	**Total**		100.00%			9.31

Investment Planning ("Accumulation" Index Weight = 25%)

% of Investment Planning Scale	Total Index Weight	Category	% of Category	% of Investment Planning Scale	Performance Score (1–10)	Total Index Weight	"WMI" Score
40%	10.00%	Is your asset allocation appropriate?					
		1. Develop coherent investment philosphy.	20%	8.00%	7	2.00%	1.40
		2. Determine the investment policy.	60%	24.00%	8	6.00%	4.80
		3. Rebalance to the investment policy.	20%	8.00%	9	2.00%	1.80
10%	2.50%	How did your actual rate of return compare with the expected rate (CPI plus target percentage)?	100%	10.00%	10	2.50%	2.50
40%	10.00%	Were your annual contributions or withdrawals at target?	100%	40.00%	10	10.00%	10.00
5%	1.25%	Was the portfolio income tax-efficient?	100%	5.00%	7	1.25%	0.88
5%	1.25%	Have you set aside enough cash for purchases to be made in the next three years?					
		1. Forecast cash needed in the next 3 years.	60%	3.00%	8	0.75%	0.60
		2. Raise cash in advance of the need.	40%	2.00%	3	0.50%	0.15
100.00%	25.00%	**Total**		100.00%			22.125

Estate Planning ("Distribution" Index Weight = 20%)

% of Estate Planning Scale	Total Index Weight	Category	% of Category	% of Estate Planning Scale	Performance Score (1-10)	Total Index Weight	"WMI" Score
40%	8.00%	Does your will match your wealth transfer wishes?					
		1. Provide detailed outline of client's objectives.	30%	12.00%	8	2.40%	1.92
		2. Do actual drafting of will (all necessary documents).	70%	28.00%	9	5.60%	5.04
25%	5.00%	Are your assets titled correctly and have you set up appropriate beneficiary designations?					
		1. Ensure all assets have correct beneficiary defined.	33%	8.35%	6	1.67%	1.00
		2. Evaluate what types of retirement accounts need to be established, split, or used for charity.	33%	8.33%	7	1.67%	1.17
		3. Review ownership of assets.	33%	8.33%	6	1.67%	1.00
15%	3.00%	Have you established and funded all necessary trusts?					
		1. Explore the use of trusts as a financial planning tool.	33%	5.00%	10	1.00%	1.00
		2. Establish those trusts deemed appropriate.	33%	5.00%	9	1.00%	0.90
		3. Maximize the funding of the trusts that require it.	33%	5.01%	7	1.00%	0.70
15%	3.00%	Do you need and have necessary planning documents (power of attorney, health care doc, living will)?					
		1. Discuss the aspects of decisionmaking powers in case of incapacitation, life support, final wishes.	50%	7.50%	10	1.50%	1.50
		2. Establish written procedures for family to execute those wishes.	50%	7.50%	7	1.50%	1.05
5%	1.00%	Have you made your desired gifts for this year?	100%	5.00%	7	1.00%	0.70
100.00%	20.00%	**Total**		100.00%			15.98

Scoring Thresholds

	Actual "WMI" Score	Perfect Score	Meets Need Score	Needs More Focus	Planning Overhaul Necessary
Asset Protection	21.24	25	21.25	16.25	Under 16.25
Disability and Income Protection	17.92	20	17	13	Under 13
Debt Management	9.31	10	8.5	6.5	Under 6.5
Investment Planning	22.125	25	21.25	16.25	Under 16.25
Estate Planning	15.98	20	17	13	Under 13
	86.575	100	85	65	Under 65

Individual "WMI" Scoring

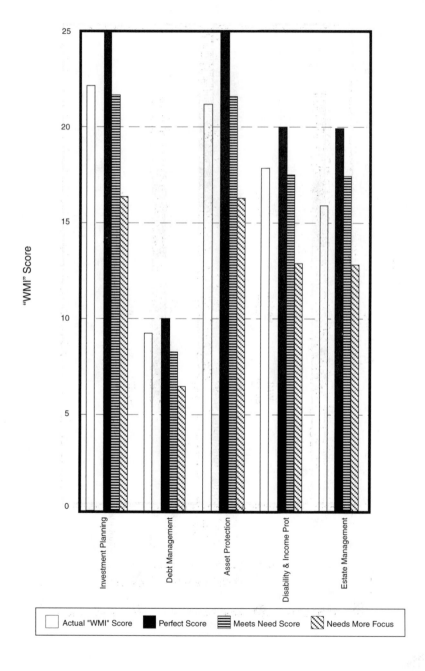

Total "WMI" Score

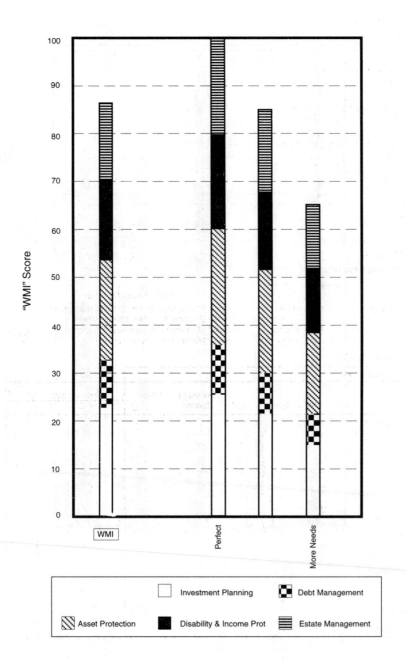

Client Workplan

ROLES/GOALS

A. *Personal/Self*
Goals: _____
_____

B. *Co-Client Relationship*
Goals: _____
_____

C. *As Parents to Your Children*
Goals: _____
_____

D. *As an Adult Child to Your Parents*
Goals: _____
_____

E. *Professional*
Goals: _____
_____

F. *Other* _____
Goals: _____
_____

SCHEDULING

I. *Planning Sessions*

Month	Planning Session	Mode of Meeting	Theme/Special Situation
May-96	1	In person	Cash Flow Management, Debt Management
August-96	2	Telephone	Asset Protection, Estate Management
November-96	3	Letter	Asset Management (year-end tax planning)
February-97	4	In person	Asset Management (year review)

II. *Other Activities*

Marketing Budget

Month	Newsletter	Dinner	Golf	Donation Charity	Other _____	Planning Sessions			
						1	2	3	4
March-96									
April-96									
May-96									
June-96									
July-96									
August-96									
September-96									
October-96									
November-96									
December-96									
January-97									
February-97									

Fact-Finding Form

Date:

	Name	Social Sec. #	Birth Date	Citizen (Yes/No)	Driver's License
Client:					
Co-Client:					
Children:					
Other Depend.:					

	Home	Business
Address #1:		
Address #2:		
City/State:		
Position:		
How Long?		
Phone #:		
Fax #:		
Cell Phone #:		
E-Mail Add:		

	Accountant	Banker	Attorney	Other Advisor
Name:				
Firm Name:				
Phone #:				
Permission to Contact:				

(Check All that Apply)

Other Information Needed

1. Copies of paystubs
2. Copies of tax return (most recent)
3. Copies of wills/trusts
4. Copies of investment statements
   - Brokerage statements
   - IRA statements
   - Retirement plan statements
5. Company benefit booklets
6. Insurance policies (life, disability, long-term care, home/auto/ umbrella)

PERSONAL INVESTMENTS

CHECKING/SAVINGS ACCOUNTS

Account Type	Location Name	Ownership (check one)			Current Balance	Credit Line & Interest Rate
		Client	Co-client	Joint		
Checking					$	$ / %
Checking					$	$ / %
Savings					$	$ / %
Money Market					$	$ / %
Other _____					$	$ / %

INVESTMENTS/NONRETIREMENT

Option One (1)
*   Provide originals or copies of all investments (we will make copies of originals and return)

Option Two (2)
*   List below those assets for which we do not have statement copies

Investment Name	Total amount Invested (Basis)	Ownership (check one)			Shares Owned	Current Balance
		Client	Co-client	Joint		
	$					$
	$					$
	$					$
	$					$
	$					$
	$					$
	$					$
	$					$
	$					$
	$					$
	$					$

PERSONAL INVESTMENTS *(continued)*

OTHER INVESTMENTS

Business Owned

Company $ Basis	Percent Ownership	Company Name	Ownership (check one)			Corp. Status (C, S, LLC, LLP)	Approx. Current Value
			Client	Co-client	Joint		
$	%						$
$	%						$

Other Nonliquid Investments

Amt Invest (Basis)	Recourse Debt	Investment Name	Ownership (check one)			Corp. Status (C, S, LLC, LLP)	Approx. Current Value
			Client	Co-client	Joint		
	yes/$						$
	yes/$						$

Information Needed (check)

☐ 1. Copy of business buy/sell agreement & financial statement.

☐ 2. Copy of last tax return for each investment (K-1 for ltd. partnership).

☐ 3. Copies of all funding vehicles (life & disability products) for company "buy/sell."

RETIREMENT INVESTMENTS

Option One (1)

* Provide originals or copies of all investments (we will make copies of originals and return)

Option Two (2)

* List below those assets for which we do not have statement copies

IRA

Investment Name	After Tax Amount	Rollover from Co. (Yes/No)	Ownership (check one)		Shares Owned	Current Balance	Pre-1986 Amount
			Client	Co-client			
	$					$	$
	$					$	$
	$					$	$
	$					$	$
	$					$	$
	$					$	$
	$					$	$
	$					$	$

PERSONAL INVESTMENTS *(continued)*

Company Retirement Plans

Investment Name	% of Salary Contrib		Hire Date Company	Ownership (check one)		Current Balance
	Company	You		Client	Co-client	
	%	%				$
	%	%				$
	%	%				$
	%	%				$
	%	%				$

Information Needed (check)

☐ 1. Copy of investment benefit statement.

☐ 2. Copy of benefit booklet showing plan attributes.

Stock Options

Option Type (NQSO, ISO, Restricted)	Grant Number	# Shares Given	Exercise Date	Ownership (check one)		Shs Exerc'd & Held	Exercise Price
				Client	Co-client		

Information Needed (check)

☐ 1. Copy of each "option agreement."

☐ 2. Copy of company provided statement of options held, vesting schedule.

USE ASSETS/LIABILITIES

HOME & OTHER PERSONAL REAL ESTATE

Terms	Primary Residence	2nd Home	3rd Home
Purchase Date			
Purchase Price	$	$	$
Current Mkt Value	$	$	$
Mortgage Amt at Last Closing	$	$	$
Current % Rate	%	%	%
Rate (Fixed, Adj–How Long?)	Adj (or) Fixed ____yrs	Adj (or) Fixed ____yrs	Adj (or) Fixed ____yrs
Mortgage term of yrs (15 or 30 yrs)	15 (or) 30 yrs	15 (or) 30 yrs	15 (or) 30 yrs
Payment:			
Prin + Int	$	$	$
Insurance	$	$	$
Taxes	$	$	$

Information Needed (check)

☐ 1. Copy of mortgage note.

☐ 2. Copy of "schedule" page of homeowners insurance.

Other Personal Assets

Asset Type	Leased or Owned	Current Value	Year Purchased	Owner	$ Insured
Car		$			$
Car		$			$
Car		$			$
Boat		$			$
Personal Property		$			$
Other _____		$			$

Liabilities

Loan Type	Current Balance Remaining	$ Payment	Interest Rate Charged	Replace Date	Term of Loan
Home					
Home Equity					
Car					
Car					
Other _____					
Other _____					
Other _____					
Other _____					

Information Needed (check)

☐ 1. Copy of mortgage note and home equity note.

INCOME—EXPENSES

Income

Source	Client	Co-Client
W-2 Salary	$	$
Bonus	$	$
When (Qtrly, Ann'l)	Mthly-Qtrly-Ann'l	Mthly-Qtrly-Ann'l
Dividends -Investments	$	$
-Company	$	$
Gifts	$	$

Information Needed (check)

☐   1.   Copy of recent pay stub.

☐   2.   Copy of company "K-1."

Expenses

Expense Type	Monthly	(or) Annual	Type of Expense Discretionary	Fixed
Food			X	
Clothing				X
School Tuition				X
Cash Card			X	
Gifts			X	
Charity			X	
Auto-Gas/Repair/ etc.				X
Car Lease Payment				X
Insur. -Life			X	
-Disability				X
-Home				X
-Auto				X
-Liability				X
-Medical				X
Furniture			X	
House Maintenance			X	
Nanny/Childcare				X
Hobbies			X	
Entertain/Dining			X	
Health Clubs			X	
Utilities			X	
Vacations				
Pets				
Home (PITI)				
Other _____				
Other _____				
Other _____				

INSURANCE COVERAGES

Life Insurance

Name of Insur. Co.	Owner	Insured	Face Amt of Life Ins.	Premium Paid/Yr.	Cash Value	Loan Amt	Bene-ficiary	Type
			$	$	$	$		
			$	$	$	$		
			$	$	$	$		
			$	$	$	$		
			$	$	$	$		
			$	$	$	$		
			$	$	$	$		
			$	$	$	$		

Information Needed (check)

☐ 1. Copy of original policy (including application which is part of policy).

☐ 2. Last 2 years "annual statements" of all policies with cash values.

☐ 3. Copy of company-provided group benefits.

Disability Insurance

Name of Insur. Co.	Insured	Monthly Benefit	Paid with Before Tax $	Premium Paid/yr	Individual or Group
		$	Yes (or) No	$	Yes (or) No
		$	Yes (or) No	$	Yes (or) No
		$	Yes (or) No	$	Yes (or) No
		$	Yes (or) No	$	Yes (or) No
		$	Yes (or) No	$	Yes (or) No
		$	Yes (or) No	$	Yes (or) No

Information Needed (check)

☐ 1. Copy of original policy (including application which is part of policy).

☐ 2. Copy of company-provided group benefits.

Home/Auto/Liability/Medical Insurance

Type	Name of Insur. Co.	Agent Name
Home		
Auto		
Liability		
Medical		
L-T Care		

Information Needed (check)

☐ 1. Copy of "schedule page" from home/auto/liability insurance.

☐ 2. Copy of company medical benefits booklet.

☐ 3. Copy of long-term care policy.

199

INDEX

Other books of interest to you from Irwin Professional Publishing and the International Association for Financial Planning. . .

THE FINANCIAL ADVISOR'S GUIDE TO DIVORCE SETTLEMENT
Helping Your Clients Make Sound Financial Decisions

Carol Ann Wilson

0-7863-0851-6

CHARITABLE REMAINDER TRUSTS
A Proven Strategy for Reducing Estate and Income Taxes Through Charitable Giving

Peter J. Fagan

0-7863-0229-1

MATURE MONEY
Marketing Financial Services to the Booming Maturity Market

Joan M. Gruber

0-7863-0971-7

WEALTH MANAGEMENT
The Financial Advisor's Guide to Investing and Managing Your Client's Assets

Harold R. Evensky

0-7863-0478-2